T0197360

# A BALANCED APPROACH
## TO
# RESTAURANT
# MANAGEMENT

# A BALANCED APPROACH
## TO
# RESTAURANT MANAGEMENT

## PETER CALDON

# A BALANCED APPROACH TO RESTAURANT MANAGEMENT

*iUniverse books may be ordered through booksellers or by contacting:*

*iUniverse*
*1663 Liberty Drive*
*Bloomington, IN 47403*
*www.iuniverse.com*
*1-800-Authors (1-800-288-4677)*

*ISBN: 978-1-5320-2714-7 (sc)*
*ISBN: 978-1-5320-2715-4 (e)*

*Library of Congress Control Number: 2017910679*

*Print information available on the last page.*

*iUniverse rev. date: 12/11/2017*

# CONTENTS

# PREFACE

Formal training in school provides a solid foundation in management theories and a safe place to get fluent in the application of management practices. However, there is no substitute for hands-on experience, where you create pilot programs to test your hypotheses and monitor and measure the results to fully assimilate what you've learned in the classroom.

Management theories and leadership styles have evolved over the years to accommodate the ever-changing challenges organizations face. Emerging theories help organizations optimize operational efficiencies, improve quality, and reduce costs, while enhancing their employees' quality of life, all of which ultimately lead to end user satisfaction.

To say it differently, we are constantly seeking new ways to engage the minds of employees and encourage them to take extraordinary actions in order to do ordinary things. Take, for example, the actions of Henry Ford, who created an assembly line in the manufacturing of cars, along with those of Steve Jobs and Bill Gates, who created devices to make everything we do easier. All three of these men were pioneers.

These transformative visionaries were able to translate thoughts to processes and procedures in order to create actionable products that have changed the way we work and live. This is what we seek to elicit from our employees daily. We wish to maximize their potential and to ensure they are mentally present on the job and able to achieve the mission and vision laid out by the owner of the business they work for.

No one set of principles or style can be effective for every situation that is present in an organization, just as no one medicine can cure all sickness. If you are diagnosed with an illness, an assessment will be made, and you'll have a range of treatment options you can rely on. The options will range from moderate to aggressive—from conservative solutions to solutions that will require lifestyle adjustments. Similarly, in food-service management, a balanced approach is best. Once you've diagnosed an issue, you can apply treatment from four perspectives—you can focus on the customer impressions, internal solutions, financial outlook, and learning and innovation. Together, these four perspectives reinforce and strengthen one another. Just as when the water level in a lake is raised all boats rise to a new level, so too will performance increase in every aspect of your organization.

A restaurant, beyond the food and beverages, is a layer of processes and procedures designed to protect the business for the long term. These procedures guide the entire team, as well as all ingredients used—from the back door and the receiving dock to the customer waiting to be served in the dining room. They play a role in everything from customer engagement to food cost to quality control and consistency.

Restaurant failure rates have remained steady; they are in the 30 percent range in the early stages and slightly higher in the later years. By sharing my experience and knowledge in food service, I aim to help you improve your business sustainability for the long term.

Managers have many demanding responsibilities. Collecting information to produce data to analyze and use intelligently is one of them. Doing so sharpens their existing skills, helps them develop new skills, and allows them to gain insights related to employees, customers, and ingredients. In short, it gives them a better understanding of food-service management.

Ultimately, *A Balanced Approach to Restaurant Management* is for anyone who is considering a career in food service, be that as an employer or an employee. Whether you plan to run a food cart, a lemonade stand, or a full-service restaurant, this book can help. It will get you to think before you act, to reflect instead of react. As a potential business owner, you will learn to assess the effectiveness of a food-service system and to implement a service blueprint that will improve your business's service-delivery processes and increase your profits. It will teach you key concepts, such as communicating instead of complaining when it comes to employee behavior and providing continuous training to change behavior that isn't working. Understanding these critical takeaways before investing your time and money is important. If you are a potential candidate for employment, *A Balanced Approach to Restaurant Management* will be a journey of discovery of your innate gifts that have yet to emerge. As you move along the wide selection of food-service choices, seek a comfortable fit for you. A career in food service will never cease to amaze you, as you will be surrounded by creative, innovative, energetic people releasing their magic with the most basic ingredients of life—food and beverages. Add the social environment and camaraderie, and balance it with a can-do attitude, and your place of work will be a satisfying destination.

This book provides a new approach to performance measurements in all aspects of the customer experience. It enables restaurants to set standards that cover their entire footprint, starting with the customer's initial contact, whether that be through social media or some other technology application or over the telephone or in person. Are your customers greeted instantly, seated fairly, and recognized immediately? Are their orders taken accurately and delivered quickly? Was their feedback gained promptly, and were their payments taken swiftly? Were they thanked graciously and invited back in a friendly manner? Similarly, were your employees screened widely, selected carefully, and oriented properly? Are they trained continuously, supervised effectively, compensated appropriately, and rewarded generously? Are they encouraged to develop internally, and when necessary, are they disciplined immediately? Measuring the actual service performance against set standards enables you to make corrections and, thus, achieve a higher performance and satisfaction level. The concept is similar to budgeting financial numbers and then making comparisons. You're actually doing the same thing with these nonfinancial measurements.

# ACKNOWLEDGMENTS

This book would not be possible without so many people and events. A casual conversation with Dr. Patrick J. Moreo at the alumni reception of the University of Nevada at Las Vegas in New York more than a decade ago, during which I expressed my desire to attend graduate school, led to him inviting me to apply to Oklahoma State University. At the time, he was director and dean of OSU's Hospitality Management Department. There, Dr. Halin Qu planted the seed of a balanced-approach-to-management model as a topic of research in my first class. Dr. Woody Woo fertilized the seeds along the way and led me to a specific focus on hospitality and full-service restaurants.

I must also acknowledge my many industry connections—you know who you are—and the long discourses we shared, testing my hypotheses.

I'm especially grateful to the Westchester Country Club, where I worked covertly to prove my hypotheses on an on-call basis, until my employers discovered my research. They embraced it, giving me more days and hours of work so that I could have a front-row seat, observing their actions and training. This provided enormous insight that enabled the completion of this book. To the new leadership team at the club, Mr. Paul Brock, general manager; Mr. Chams B. Mansour, director of food and beverage; Mr. Billy Panagiotopoulos, director of sales and catering; Mr. Brian Falasco, director of banquets; Mr. Moises Martinez, banquet manager; and

Mr. Jean St. Hilare, executive steward, thank you for your time. The opportunity to compare and contrast leadership styles and the skills of managers from past to present was priceless. The careful attention to detail I witnessed evoked the passion, vibrancy, and snappiness of a time gone by, when style and grace, not visually driven social media, were the norm.

Most importantly, I am grateful to my wife, AnneMarie, for bearing with me and my seeming absentmindedness (which was really my singular focus on the balanced-approach methodology).

To Vaughn and Nigel, my two sons, thank you for pushing me over the finish line when feedback from the content and editorial evaluation was constant and seemed to never end.

Although I never asked, I believe the depth and broad base of my experience across many segments of the food-service industry had something to do with my acceptance at OSU. The department seemed to be waiting with a predetermined topic of research that fit my experience. It was the perfect intersection in my career.

# A NEW STYLE OF MANAGEMENT

Having it all and wanting it now is in vogue. But balancing career, parenthood, wellness, and your finances in today's workplace environment is a challenge. In the field of food-service management, managers have to balance many things. Among these are evolving dining habits, including customers' rising expectations of a wide selection of healthy alternative dishes and an increase in celebratory occasions to dine. Food-service managers need to implement improved operational processes that reduce cycle time and to anticipate the rising costs of labor, ingredients, and energy. They must create an environment that enables continuous learning and innovation in order to keep abreast of ever-changing technology, equipment, and trends; this means continually training and developing the skills of employees to match rising expectations.

Management styles have evolved over time, away from the hard-driving type A corporate executive of the seventies, whose only goal was to increase sales at any cost. When a major midwestern manufacturing company went bankrupt even with yearly sales increases, the focus changed, and controlling cost became the new mantra in the eighties. As we have learned, from the famous "Where's the beef?" Wendy's commercial, increasing prices while reducing portion size does not create customer value; accordingly, the focus shifted again to customer expectation and satisfaction in the early nineties.

We learned that not all customers have the same needs and expectations, so segmentation into bite-size niches of menu type, service delivery, and location became the order of the day.

On reflection, the above example's emphasis was on the financial segment, sales, cost of sales, and then customer service. It was the conventional thinking at the time. Now, we strive for a balanced approach to managing our businesses—one that includes innovation and learning and internal cycle processes.

Robert Kaplan and David Norton, observing and working with Fortune 100 companies, found that senior executives do not rely on one set of performance measures to the exclusion of others. They discovered that no single measure can provide a clear target or focus attention on the critical areas of the business. Managers want a balanced look at both financial and operational measures. The Balanced Scorecard (BSC) system was founded on that insight.[1]

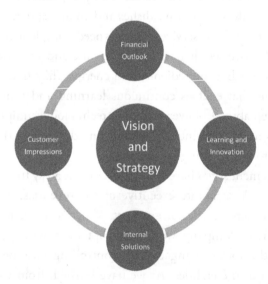

Diagram #1: A Balance Approach from four perspectives

In food service, there are four distinct areas to manage—customer impressions, internal solutions, financial outlook, and learning and innovation. The division of management into four parts shines a light on problem areas. By focusing on each area individually, managers can then strategically connect one segment to the others. As a result, each segment becomes more manageable, as its objective is aligned to the overall vision of the operation (as indicated in diagram 1).

Measures can now be developed to indicate how well each segment is performing compared to the whole. Every action in each segment contributes to an objective and, in turn, to an overall vision. A balanced approach, then, can be applied. Managers must always take action and make decisions based on an overall vision, which is translated to a mission, for each segment. Easier said than done, you may think. You'll find examples later on to show, tell, and inspire.

In times of change, this strategy remains focused on objectives, not control. Plans of actions can always change in the short term to meet long-term goals. To succeed in this changing environment, managers must apply their time equally and effectively among the competing segments of the business. Only then will they be able to balance equal and opposing forces, both internally and externally.

Peruse any company's annual reports or the pages of business and professional journals, and you'll see that the word *balance*—"on balance," "balanced approach," "balance sheet," "to balance," and so on—comes up quite often. Even US President Barack Obama, in one of his State of the Union speeches used the term. He was describing his strategy for the US Department of Education, which would hold the department accountable with a balance scorecard (BSC) approach.

Bruce White, the legendary chairman and CEO of White Lodging Services, has had twenty-five years of success. In an interview with Bruce Serlen of *Hotel Business* in March 2011, after being given the Award for Excellence and Inspiration at the Hunter Conference in Atlanta, White stated, "The challenge as we continue to grow and become a larger organization is to still get better." He went on, "Most people think that when you get bigger, you become less responsive to your guests or owners, yet we have always said that we were only going to get bigger if we could get better and become more significant. That is happening now without a doubt. Our balanced scorecard, our owner feedback, every way we have to measure performance has just become better and better."[2]

Multiple literature sources give various definitions for the term *balance*. A few include, "a stable state characterized by the cancellation of all forces by equal opposing forces," "an even distribution of weight enabling someone or something to remain steady or upright," "a condition in which different elements are equal or in correct portions," "to offset or compare the value of one thing with another, and finally, "something left over."

Here, we will use all of these definitions appropriately. The second definition—an even distribution of weight to remain steady and upright—best describes the situation of restaurant operation. Four specific areas must be balanced, and their weight must be evenly distributing to keep the business steady and upright and achieving financial success (see diagram 2).

| Weight | Measure | On Target | Current Period Measure | Rating | Rolling 3 Periods Measure | Rating | Year To Date Measure | Rating |
|---|---|---|---|---|---|---|---|---|
| 25% | **CUSTOMER IMPRESSIONS** | | | | | | | |
| 25% | Customer satisfaction survey | 95 | 95.9 | | 95.65 | | 97.4 | |
| 25% | **INTERNAL SOLUTIONS** | | | | | | | |
| 5% | Peak: % of customers served > 25 | 5 | 4.9 | | 5 | | 5 | |
| 5% | Off Peak: % of customers served > 20 | 5 | 4.85 | | 4.99 | | 4.99 | |
| 5% | Peak: Additional purchases > 7min | 5 | 4.9 | | 4.98 | | 4.98 | |
| 5% | Off Peak: Additional purchases > 5min | 5 | 4.8 | | 4.97 | | 4.97 | |
| 5% | Meal Rejection rate % | 5 | 4.92 | | 4.96 | | 4.96 | |
| 25% | **FINANCIAL OUTLOOK** | | | | | | | |
| 5% | Sales v Budget | 100 | 105.5 | | 105.6 | | 106.8 | |
| 5% | Sales v LY | 100 | 103.2 | | 102.5 | | 103.1 | |
| 5% | Covers v Budget | 100 | 106 | | 106 | | 106.5 | |
| 5% | Covers v LY | 100 | 103.2 | | 102.5 | | 103.1 | |
| 5% | Employee Sales v Budget | 100 | 101 | | 100 | | 103.1 | |
| 25% | **GROWTH & INNOVATION** | | | | | | | |
| 5% | Employee Turnover rate | 50 | 90 | | 175.4 | | 199.9 | |
| 5% | Training index | 100 | 98 | | 95 | | 90 | |
| 5% | Capital improvement % of revenue | 3 | 1 | | 1 | | 1 | |
| 5% | % of new revenue stream | 100 | 105.5 | | 105.6 | | 106.8 | |
| 5% | % of improvement over LY | 100 | 102 | | 103 | | 102 | |
| 100% | **OVERALL SCORE** | | | | | | | |

Diagram #2: A Balance Scorecard

When the mission of each segment is aligned with the business's overall vision statement and when equal weight is applied to all four segments, the system outperforms expectations, and there is something left over for owners and shareholders.

In order to maintain a sustainable management style—one that can withstand the wide variety of thinkers and influences that sway food service yearly, not to mention the monthly assortment of flavors—food-service managers must take advantage of the balanced approach. Doing so will allow them to adjust the weight they're giving to each of the four food-service segments, redistributing their energy when needed to confront a specific threat internally or externally and maintaining a steady, smooth flow of operations.

Many industries have adopted this approach to performance measurement. You'll find the BSC approach in banking, oil and gas, health care, hospitality, insurance, manufacturing, and technology. Some studies estimate that 40 percent of Fortune 500 companies have incorporated some elements of this balanced approach into their management systems.

In the hospitality industry, the lodging segment was an early adopter of the balanced scorecard, starting at the corporate level before drilling down to individual properties.

Let us now have a look at how the balanced scorecard framework might apply to the operations of a full-service restaurant. This discussion is based on a review of literature examining the application of the BSC strategy in health care services, oil and gas, financial services, manufacturing, insurance, and the lodging segment of the hospitality industries, along with discussions and interviews with general managers of national chain restaurants and my own work experience across many segments of the food-service industry.

A *full-service restaurant*, for our purposes, is defined as a sit-down eatery, where food is prepared and served directly to the customer's table. These establishments offer a wide selection of food, sell alcoholic beverages, provide takeout delivery, present live entertainment, have outdoor seating and valet parking, and may have a dress code policy. See diagram 3 to review the organizational structure of such an establishment.

## Organizational Structure of a Full-Service Restaurant

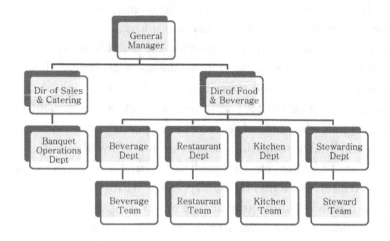

Diagram # 3: Organization chart for Full Service Restaurant

We will now walk through the process of building a blueprint for a balanced scorecard framework for a full-service restaurant. This approach represents a significant change from the traditional mind-set of the food-service industry, in which high expectations of being the best are stated without the corresponding human resources, technology, and financial fit needed to meet those lofty goals. Ambiguous statements about things like being the best, serving the freshest food, and providing top-notch service (or even "I can cook, and everybody got to eat right," as one owner said to me) contribute to restaurant failures. And failure rates are high. A group of researchers, led by Dr. H. G. Parsa, who taught at Ohio State University in 2005 and is now at the University of Denver's School of Business, studied these rates and reported, "Just under 30% of restaurants closed or changed ownership during the first year of operations. This is true with both independent and chain operated with slight variation of turnover rate. By the end of the third year it's 60% again with miniscule variation of turnover rate. This pattern has being holding true for the previous two decades."[3]

While serving on the board of the Ohio Restaurant Association, Dr. Parsa came across a foolproof source for learning exactly how long restaurants remained in business—the health department. "Every restaurant has to be inspected by the health department before it opens, and the license has to be renewed every single year. The only time they don't renew you is when you're closed. I thought, 'Wow, there we go—when a restaurant opens I know it because of the license, and when it closes I know because it's not renewed.' The research was done credibly, scientifically." Data was collected over four years from among 1,400 restaurants.

Never forget to check where data comes from. Case in point, I once listened to a colleague's presentation on health care. He was vice president of a major health care provider in New York. At the end of the presentation, I made my way up front to ask him where he'd gotten all the statistics he'd quoted in his speech. He told me he "made it up." In this age of information and big data collection and reality television shows that cover the full spectrum of food service—from cooking, drinking, and managing to designing and consulting—it is important to know where information comes from and how it was obtained. Pay attention to whether the data you're evaluating comes from a primary source, a secondary source, or a bubble gum wrapper or fortune cookie insert.

The size of a study's sample population adds to its credibility. The larger the sample size, the more able the study is to generalize its findings to a targeted industry upon analysis of the data collected. Television shows offer just a glimpse of the real world of food service as entertainment and should come with the following labels: Do not try this at your restaurant. Restaurants are not all the same. Check with your consultant, doctor, banker, and divorce attorney before starting this journey. What you see does not guarantee your success. Not responsible for loss of family ties.

# 2

# A FOUNDATION FOR SUCCESS

First, we'll talk about the significance of the scorecard, and then we'll build our blueprint by including each of the four food-service segments. Next, we'll show the linkages—that is, how continuous training that ensures employees are constantly learning and innovating leads to customer satisfaction leads to improvement of internal cycle time leads to financial success. Yes, your employees, not the customer, are the drivers of your success. Get ready to reset your thinking.

Next up, we'll discuss ways of communicating the new strategy to department managers, who in turn translate the vision statement into a mission. From this, a plan of action is born and passed on to individual employees so that their daily actions will be aligned with the company's objectives.

Finally, using feedback from employees, customers, and suppliers, we'll monitor the external environment to implement new strategies for continuous improvement in operational efficiencies—making changes in equipment and technology and training employees for personal growth and development in order to achieve long-term success.

## The relevance of the balanced scorecard

The balanced scorecard can be custom-built for any restaurant type. Primarily, a BSC strategy is a method and plan of action chosen to bring about the achievement of a desired goal. Secondly, it enables the planning and marshaling of resources for their most efficient and effective use based on a prioritization of goals. Next, it allows managers to build a self-directed team full of goal-oriented members all striving to achieve a desired outcome. Standards and measures are created to hold each team member accountable for their contribution to the team goal. The combination of a plan of action, the application of resources where they are most needed, and supporting employees in taking whatever action is necessary to arrive at their goal is the heart and soul of the balance scorecard. Another distinctive element of the system is that it changes to suit the conditions employees face each meal period, day of the week, and catered event. It takes into account likes and dislikes and hard-to-please customers, makes control a remote action for managers to handle. These short-term, actionable steps build fitness and increase the possibility of long-term success. More importantly, managers release the traditional responsibility for one specific area, becoming, instead, part of a team of managers working together across multiple areas to accomplish the company's goals.

The customers' footprint as a whole pie can be sliced into four pieces, to mirror the restaurant's four operational segments. The first, customer impressions at the moment of truth contact point, goes along with customer service. The food and beverage choices reflect the internal solutions. Payment is a replica of your financial outlook. And the invitation to return is parallel to the learning and innovation segment.

Understanding how the four segments of a customer's experience, just like the four segments of a restaurant, come together to complete the whole can help managers discover that protecting one's own functional area to the detriment of another serves no useful purpose.

Time becomes more valuable, and managers focus more on execution of standards, measuring employee performance, and studying the overall impact of both on department goals.

The BSC keeps your restaurant looking fresh and thinking forward.

## Building a balanced scorecard

Each restaurant must follow its own salient path to building a BSC that is appropriate for its market segment, service delivery, menu, and location. To fully develop a BSC requires a deep understanding of the four pillars of the design. A restaurant's Customer Impressions , Financial Outlook, Internal Solutions, and Learning and Innovation must guide the building of its owner's vision.

Here is an example of a vision statement and a mission statement, which we will be using as we build out the scorecard:

### Vision

When our customers walk in the door, they are greeted by a wow atmosphere; subtle Caribbean music; and a friendly, courteous staff, instantly setting the mood for relaxation and fun.

We offer a refined experience to large groups celebrating special occasions and to individual customers without delays in seating, recognition, and delivery of service.

The lighting, tableware arrangements, atmosphere, and decorations all encourage our customers to relax, let go of their concerns, and open up to new taste sensations. We provide exceptional service.

When customers are finished, we take care of their checks quickly and efficiently. They leave happy, satisfied, and with the desire to return for one more bite of our wonderful food.

## Mission

- to sell delicious and remarkable food and drinks that meet the highest standards of quality, freshness, and seasonality and combine both modern/creative and traditional Caribbean styles of cooking

- to consistently provide our customers with impeccable service by demonstrating warmth, graciousness, efficiency, knowledge, professionalism, and integrity in our work

- to have every customer who comes through our doors leave impressed and excited to come back again

- to create and maintain a restaurant that is comprehensive and exceptional in its attention to every detail of operation

- to provide all who work with us a friendly, cooperative, and rewarding environment that encourages growth and long-term, satisfying employment

- to keep our concept fresh, exciting, and on the cutting edge of the hospitality and entertainment industry

- to be a giving member of the community and to use our restaurant to improve the quality of life in our community and offer a fair return on investment to our stakeholders

## Something for every employee to rally behind

The owner and the general manager, along with a consultant, interview managers to obtain their input on the company's strategic objectives. To provide an external perspective to the deliberations, customers, suppliers, and shareholders are interviewed about their expectations. A tentative proposal for the balanced scorecard mission is documented.

Next, a senior management group meets in a workshop with managers to debate the proposed mission and strategy statements until a consensus is reached. Then, after defining the key success factors, the group formulates a preliminary scorecard, which contains operational measures for reaching strategic objectives.

The facilitator reviews, consolidates, and documents the output from the first workshop and seeks opinions on strategies for implementing the scorecard. A second workshop is held. This time, senior managers meet with the next two levels of middle managers, assistant managers, and supervisors and/or team leaders. This group debates the organizational vision, the strategy statements, and the tentative scorecard. Participants, working in groups, comment on proposed measures and start to develop implementation plans. Senior managers usually set the financial and customer objectives and measures, leaving it to the middle managers to determine the operation's internal business processes, as well as strategies for achieving the learning and feedback objectives and measures.

A total of five measures for each perspective are ideal. However, implementing three measures to begin with, as diagram 4 indicates, and then adding another when one has been accomplished and maintained, might better keep employees freshly motivated. In addition, this strategy will avoid their feeling overwhelmed with the demands of meeting measurement standards and, consequently, neglecting customer service.

Finally, senior managers meet a third time to come to a final consensus on the vision, objectives, and measurement strategies. The team must agree on an implementation program, which should include how the scorecard will be communicated to employees, how it will be integrated into the management philosophy, and how an information system to support it will be developed. This program must link the measures to databases and information systems and communicate the BSC approach throughout the organization. As a result, an entirely new information system is created—a system that links top-level business metrics all the way down to the dining room and bar. It is during this deliberation that the successful implementation of the BSC is determined for the long-term success of the restaurant.

Now is a great opportunity for the department managers to present to the group what the new approach will look like and how it will impact the department's operational efficiency before communicating the new strategy to the employees. Creating a simple, straightforward marketing plan that can be presented both visually and verbally will greatly increase employees' ability and desire to buy in to the new system. You can, to an extent, foolproof your operation through repetition. Where constant communication in all its glorious forms takes precedence, employees rarely get it wrong.

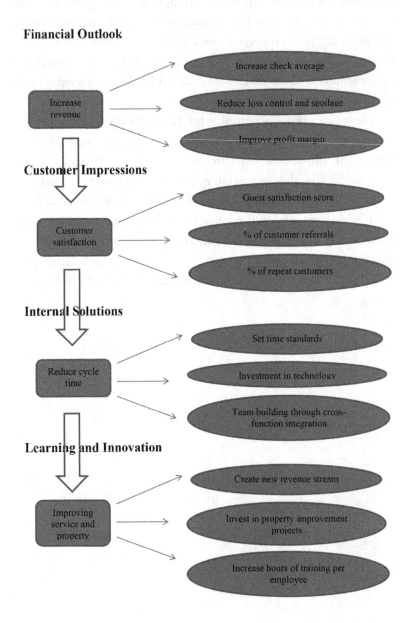

**Financial Outlook**

Increase revenue

Increase check average

Reduce loss control and spoilage

Improve profit margin

**Customer Impressions**

Customer satisfaction

Guest satisfaction score

% of customer referrals

% of repeat customers

**Internal Solutions**

Reduce cycle time

Set time standards

Investment in technology

Team building through cross-function integration

**Learning and Innovation**

Improving service and property

Create new revenue stream

Invest in property improvement projects

Increase hours of training per employee

Diagram #4: BSC Goals and Measures

# 3

# COMMUNICATION AND LINKAGES

Oral and written communications are the two prime ways we share information. Nonverbal communication is important too. Used correctly, body language, mirroring, facial expression, and eye contact can support what is being communicated. Eye contact shows you are interested, your facial expression tells how you feel, mirroring a person's body position is proof you are in sync with him or her, and body language makes evident your like or dislike of a situation.

We use each of these methods of communication every day. Which one you choose depends on who your audience is. No one method will get through to all. Getting to know your audience, in this case your employees, and how you want them to use the information, will determine how you share it.

When it comes to verbal communication, keeping it short and sweet is key. Present information that can be easily memorized and easily repeated. Make sure it is a call to action. Here are two examples:

- The culture of oral communication rewards redundancy. When an audience can't go back and consult a text, speakers must guard against distraction and confusion. Repetition is one useful technique, and Donald J. Trump is a master of it. Consider the remarks he made during a March debate in the 2016 presidential campaign: "I'm a leader. I'm a leader. I've always been a leader. I've never had any problem leading people. If I say do it, they're going to do it. That's what leadership is all about." Mr. Trump was making the point that his experience as a business leader is transferable to his capability as a political leader. As such, he repeated the key term *leader* in order to make his message—he is a leader--stick.

- The second example also comes from Mr. Trump during the 2016 presidential campaign. He never referred to his opponents by their real names. He never said "Ted Cruz," "Marco Rubio," or "Hillary Clinton"; rather, he spoke of "Lyin' Ted," "Little Marco," and "Crooked Hillary." These endlessly repeated epithets packed extra information into small, instantly memorable packets, easily remembered and repeated.

The importance of communication cannot be denied. Using effective communication skills is crucial to relationships and to success at work.

We can now focus on communicating the vision to department employees, so that their behavior and actions align with department goals, which in turn are aligned with company goals. As customer satisfaction is paramount in achieving company goals, the challenge is translating and communicating to the back-of-the-house and office employees the stated missions:

- to sell delicious and remarkable food and drinks that meet the highest standards of quality, freshness, and seasonality and combine both modern/creative and traditional Caribbean styles of cooking

- to consistently provide our customers with impeccable service by demonstrating warmth, graciousness, efficiency, knowledge, professionalism, and integrity in our work

- to have every customer who comes through our doors leave impressed and excited to come back again

- to create and maintain a restaurant that is comprehensive and exceptional in its attention to every detail of operation

- to provide all who work with us a friendly, cooperative, and rewarding environment that encourages growth and long-term, satisfying employment

- to keep our concept fresh, exciting, and on the cutting edge of the hospitality and entertainment industry

- to be a giving member of the community and to use our restaurant to improve the quality of life in our community and offer a fair return on investment to stakeholders

Keep in mind that back-of-the-house and office employees might never encounter the customers for whom they plan, purchase, store, prep, and cook. For people they'll never meet, these employees assemble delicious and remarkable food and drinks that meet the highest standards of quality, freshness, and seasonality and deliver them to the dining room or bar or packaged to go.

Change is inevitable. Change is challenging. When it comes to implementing change, the degree of difficulty will depend on the gap between what it is now and what will be moving forward. That gap determines the amount of available flexibility—in other words, your team members' ability to shake loose from me to we quickly. We're talking about the aptitude for changing an attitude. We want to go from mottos such as "This is how we always do it" and "I would like to help you, but this is our policy" to statements like "How can I make your evening special?" and "I will be delighted to get that for you." Continuous learning, like change, is unavoidable. The more you learn, the more you do and the more you change. To reduce the uncertainty of the what's-next syndrome affecting your team, you must create a climate of service wherein improving and evolving becomes a cultural norm.

In order to adopt a new attitude, encourage flexibility, close the gap quickly, and cross the bridge to a new level of customer-service teamwork, increasing communication is paramount. Any gap in communication will be filled with employees' innuendo, gossip, and rumormongering. Here is where managers' emotional intelligence comes into play. It is important to maintain an even keel, remain calm, keep emotions in check, and always think before speaking. Stay on message—change is here, and we are all in this together. Change builds organizational muscle, enabling the restaurant to get to the next level so the next change will be an easy lift.

To create a climate of service, you have to hire people with a disposition to serve. To develop a solution-oriented culture in your organization you must have a standard operating procedure (SOP) manual that guides your ingredients and personnel through the process of creating "delicious and remarkable food."

The same goes for next two points of the mission—"to consistently provide our customers with impeccable service by demonstrating warmth, graciousness, efficiency, knowledge, professionalism, and integrity in our work" and "to have every customer who comes through our doors leave impressed and excited to come back again." Then, when you fall short of this new level of expectation, it will be easy to identify, correct, and improve the process. You'll simply trace steps back to see where and with whom the slippage occurred.

To drive the vision down to the department's mission and bring employees' actions into alignment, create a dashboard of information with which to communicate. Showing employees the linkage between segments of the business will enable them to translate new expectations into action. The dashboard will consist of financial meters, customer-service pictorials, internal improvement diagrams, and feedback and improvement gauges, as well as training and development signage.

Casting further light on this transformation, I am reminded of an experience I encountered while subbing as a math teacher at a junior high school in Queens. When I walked into the classroom, I saw that every surface area was covered with informational posters, signs, and diagrams. These materials explained everything from decimals, fractions, the basic operational order of equations, divisors, quotients, and dividends to the importance of being calm and showing your work.

Wow! *An a-ha moment*, I thought. How can children not learn math in this environment? It put me in mind of the cliché "Build it, and they will come." In this case, create a learning environment, and they will learn. You and I know that is not always the case. There are too many variables to make that a completely true statement. Some will learn. Others won't, even with great teaching skills and class management.

In food service, the same is true. Even with all the signage, posters, checklist diagrams, and verbal coaching, there will always be a Sally who would like to punish the organization for shaking things up. She does not want to change. She does not want to move from her comfort zone. Eventually, she will have to move on. Others, meanwhile, will embrace the opportunity to show their true selves, which were hidden under the old way—whatever that way was, be it "my way or the highway" or "ask before you act."

In other words, it's important to reduce the stress of change to the new mind-set—one where statements like "I would be delighted to get it for you" are the order of the day. First, managers must be aware that, while the storm of change is passing, stress is increasing for the employees caught in the middle. Therefore, clear and distinct boundaries must be established. Only then will your employees be empowered and energetic and will teamwork come to the forefront. This will reverse or at least bring to a minimum the amount of "ask before you act" situations. And will not put the performance standard (established so your restaurant will be profitable) at risk. As the winds of change continue to blow and cause some damage, the Sallys of the workplace should be part of the cleanup to avoid a lengthy rebuilding process.

By doing so, managers will show that they are, indeed, creating a new environment, in which customers are consistently provided impeccable service by employees' demonstration of warmth, graciousness, efficiency, knowledge, professionalism, and integrity. They'll demonstrate their desire to ensure that every customer leaves "impressed and excited to come back again." And moreover, they'll show that they *mean it*.

\* \* \*

The next step to complete the linkage and to tighten the communication loop among the departments is cross-training employees in at least two other departments. As an example, dining room employees may train alongside caterers and bartenders. Other good combinations could include pairing the culinary department with the purchasing and receiving department, sanitation and maintenance employees with culinary specialists, or the sales team with the human resources and accounting department.

Selection for cross-training should be based on which employees can assimilate seamlessly among the many ethnicities that are predominant in our service industry. Let's be honest here; just go to your cafeteria and observe the informal circles that sit together during employee breaks and meal periods. In my experience, the Vietnamese employees sit at one table, the Latinos at another, the Eastern Europeans at the next, African Americans at the next, and so on with whatever other ethnic groups you employ. And there is always an Anthony or a Mary who transcends the groups with his or her charisma—a presence that pulls the various circles together. Anthony's and Mary's appeal will assist the transformation process. Train them and other employees will easily model the actions you expect moving forward. Their drawing power will get all to follow their lead. The next time you want to improve personal appearance, ensuring all arrive at work with their shoes polished and shining and armed with the tools of the trade (wine key, lighter, pen, and table crumbier), just let Anthony and Mary be your models.

To bring an external perspective to your team, have employees dine at restaurants in your competitive market set. Encourage them to share their experiences at pre-meal meetings. This will sharpen their skill sets and give them the advantage of comparison. It will help them encourage customers to choose to dine at your establishment, rather than the competitor's.

By cross-training and encouraging comparison, your team will become stronger. They'll have an edge that will ensure they are better prepared to deliver exceptional service all the time. Now get ready to create measures for performances in the four areas of operations.

# 4

# CUSTOMER-SERVICE IMPRESSION

What your customers hear, see, touch, smell, taste, and learn is the sum total of their experience with your restaurant. The customers' impression is created every second they are connected with your restaurant in person or online. In person, customers' impression may be influenced by the flower garden landscaped along the path to the entrance, the music that punctuates the silence as they open the door, or the broad-smiled greeting they receive from the impeccably dressed host inside. Before long, they'll have engaged with the waiter, the food, the beverages, the manager, the amenities, and the cashier, and then they'll disappear into thin air, leaving you hoping they'll return. That short visit was your opportunity to ensure that someone who came from wherever doesn't disappear into thin air—that someone who came in as a stranger leaves as a friend of yours, the restaurant, and the cash register.

It is this experience that we'll focus on in this chapter, showing the meaningful interrelationship among the many variables in the customer experience. We will narrow our focus down to food quality, service, and decor because these aspects emerge as the top three in all the available dining literature. Each aspect has additional components. They are the three critical success factors.

Food quality attributes include the following:

- taste

- texture

- color

- variety

- presentation

Service attributes include the following:

- recognition

- waiting time to be seated

- waiting time to be served

- order accuracy

- friendly employees to engage customers and cultivate relationships

Decor attributes include the following:

- lighting

- furniture and fixtures

- tapestry

- space

How do we measure for all the variables in food quality, service, and decor? The soft variables in all three categories can be bundled together to form an overall customer satisfaction score. Balance can become the operating standards to be measured. For example, waiting time (when it comes to a customer being greeted, being seated, having his or her order taken, and served) can be grouped together.

When and how these variables are measured is just as important as why. Feedback surveys from which the customer satisfaction score is derived and measured should be done within two days of a customer's visit. Allowing time for the customer to digest (pardon the pun) the experience will ensure a more objective and less emotional response, as opposed to an on-the-spot feedback channel. This applies to all forms of feedback channels, including social media (post a review); brief questionnaires; or, for better or worse, the waiter, manager, or cashier asking, "How was everything, Mr. Jones?" on the customer's way out. Do you really think Mr. Jones has time to tell you about everything? As a matter of fact, Mr. Jones may find the question irrelevant and insulting on his way out. After all, you had all the time in the world during his dining experience to learn along the way whether he was satisfied with his choices of food and beverage and how long he had to wait to be seated, have his order taken, and get served. At this point, he'll have already made up his mind, and with a sarcastic smile on his face, he'll nod his head without further comment and disappear into the thin air of the competitor.

Immediate feedback solicitations should be simpler. For example, let's say the question to Mr. Jones on his way out had been "How was Marco tonight?" Mr. Jones would have known that your enquiry was about service. You'd likely get a fuller response, something like "Oh great guy—I like him" or "What a character" or "Friendly, didn't know he does wax sculpturing." What a difference a question makes. Mr. Jones's response tells you that Marco executed all the operating procedures standards for service and hit a home run in the wiggle room for engagement. Feedback like this supports, confirms, and compliments other mediums, helping you move toward an overall customer satisfaction score.

The rationale for waiting a couple days for feedback can be illustrated by considering people's emotions when related to purchasing a new car. In the showroom the cars look impressive. They're shiny and seem to have all the bells and whistles. You take in the smell of the interior leather and the quiet sound of the powerful engine. You enjoy the feeling of comfort as you sit on a heated and massage-enabled armchair driver seat, complete with gauges, meters, icons, and buttons to get you connected to everything except your favorite morning coffee. What's not to like about your new car?

What if, the next day, the wiper blade falls off when you activate the button to clear the windshield as the rain begins to fall? What will you think? How will you feel about the salesman, the company, the car, and the money you spent?

Got the point? With one differentiator, the total experience changes. When a customer's impression lingers for two days and remains positive, if you ask me, that is one very satisfied customer. And you're on the way to fulfilling your mission of ensuring every customer who comes through the doors leaves impressed and excited to come back again and again.

Whereas you can take the car back to the dealer to get the wiper fixed, you'll have no such luck in the food-service business. Consider the mission of a homeland security agency. Every day, agents are tasked with preventing just one person, one time to take the opportunity to cause massive damage to the homeland. The same concept applies in a restaurant. You have to put in place measurable processes, procedures, standards, and policies to prevent any customer experience from blowing up and causing massive damage to your brand.

Think about the Chipotle restaurant chain, a recent example of this principle. Consider Bruce White's words: "The challenge as we continue to grow and become a larger organization is to still get better." White also noted, "Most people think that when you get bigger you become less responsive to your guests or owners, yet we have always said that we were only going to get bigger if we could get better and become more significant." This was a lesson Chipotle learned the hard way. You get bigger and better with a balanced approach to management and with a scorecard to keep score, if you will, on the many details necessary to run a smooth and efficient operation. Such balance is critical to your success.

Chipotle's problems began in August 2015, when more than two hundred people came down with the norovirus after eating at one of its restaurants in Simi Valley, California. The same month, sixty-four people who ate at one of twenty-two Chipotle restaurants in Minnesota and Wisconsin got salmonella poisoning.

But it wasn't until November, when the company announced it had closed a string of stores across the Pacific Northwest because of E. coli contamination that investors began to flee. The next month, there was another E. coli problem in the Midwest. And in February 2016, some two hundred people got sick with norovirus after eating at a Chipotle in Boston.

"Part of the thing that was so devastating was because there were multiple incidents, and so it may have looked like we were out of control," said Steve Ells, Chipotle founder and co–chief executive. "We had good food safety standards in place—but were they good enough to ensure something like this wouldn't happen give the momentum of our business and that we rely on fresh ingredients prepared on the spot? Maybe not."

Michelle Greenwald, a marketing professor at Columbia University, said, "You can be a pioneer in the market and get surpassed by other things." Chipotle's food safety problems coincided with its introduction of new concepts like Cava Grill and Sweetgreen.

Chipotle announced that its sales in stores open for at least a year had tumbled by 23.6 percent, compared with the same period the previous year. It was the third consecutive quarter that the company's same-store sales had dropped.

Profits for the quarter that ended June 30, 2016, were $25.6 million, down from $140.2 million in the same period in the prior year, when Chipotle had its first food safety problem.

Let me translate using basketball analogies. Chipotle was like the Golden State Warriors team of 2016, which lost to the Cleveland Cavaliers after leading three games to one in the championship finals of the National Basketball Association. They had two of the best shooters in the game—Stephen Curry and Klay Thompson—and a defensive specialist in Draymond Green. They were breaking records, including most games won in a season and most nearly everything else, rewriting the record books. Like the Golden State Warriors, Chipotle was breaking records in same-store sales open for at least a year within their segment of the restaurant industry. The company was expanding everywhere, increasing its customer count, and getting repeat customers. Stock prices were virtually going through the roof. Like the Golden State Warriors, Chipotle was looking ahead to the playoffs and to becoming champions. In basketball, you cannot pass the ball forward until you receive it and hold it in your hands. In other words, you have to have the ball to pass it. Chipotle's management focused on the company's new concepts (like Cava Grill and Sweetgreen), looking forward, and took their eyes off the ball. And their employees dropped the pass in food safety practices. A lesson can be learned from Chipotle's example: "You practice not till you get it right but until you never do it wrong."

Great hand-eye coordination is another good basketball metaphor. Food-service business owners must keep their hands in the business with an eye to the future.

Let's look at Mr. Ells's words again, which he said in hindsight. "We had good food safety standards in place—but were they good enough to ensure something like this wouldn't happen given the momentum of our business and that we rely on fresh ingredients prepared on the spot? Maybe not." It is not unusual for employees of fast-growing companies to become desensitized. They turn down and tune out the best practices that were critical to their success in handling fresh ingredients, especially meats and poultry, because of the scale and increased workload. They're busy trying to keep up with their growth and development of new stores and increased customer count. Combine that with reduced supervision, record keeping, and inspection (employees will always cut corners to keep pace) and you've created a perfect storm—in this case, for E. coli contamination and the norovirus.

Perception is reality in business. So it's not clear why Mr. Ells seemed surprised. The incidents did, in fact, occur throughout the country. They weren't isolated even to, say, in the Northwest or Northeast. Incidents occurred in Minnesota and Wisconsin in the Midwest as well. It was a systemic failure in the food supply chain.

Now, all of these aspects of the business are overseen by a food safety leader in each restaurant, a new position. Overreaction will not recover customers' confidence. "You have to build a culture of food safety so employees become unconsciously competent in it," said Robert Gravani, who teaches food safety at Cornell University, when he heard about what Chipotle was doing.

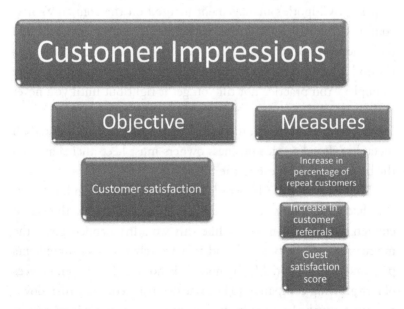

Diagram #5: Customer Impression Objective and Measures

You measure to compare an action to a standard. That way, you can see how often the action *was* performed in comparison to the amount of times it *could have been* performed. As an example, let's say you set a standard of answering the telephone by the third ring. You call the number ten times a day, and it is answered on the second ring every time. You have achieved the telephone answering standard 100 percent of the time.

It's important to note that you cannot measure everything. If you do, your employees will become focused on measurement performance and not on customer satisfaction. Although customer satisfaction is indeed paramount, and you have set standards to achieve the desired result, you have to leave wiggle room for individual performance. Consider, for example, issues with today's education, where test scores, instead of students' learning, have become the barometer of teachers' performance. Students are at the mercy of policy makers, who desire test scores. And the result is test takers, rather than well-rounded students. As the saying goes, you measure what's critical to your success and manage what you measure.

In each area, let's select three variables to measure. For our customer impression section, we'll look at customer satisfaction score, customer referrals, and percentage of repeat customers (see diagram 5). Satisfaction scores will come from customer survey questionnaires. The responses relate to a variety of attributes and will relate to food quality, service, and decor—our three established areas of focus. To ensure valid measurements, it's necessary to make sure the questionnaire actually covers all aspects of the variable that is being examined. Only then will the survey predict what it claims to predict. Survey responses should be collected over a period of time to generate a large enough response to be confident in the results. Then you can narrow it down to just three questions, as some companies who have being doing the long-form questionnaires for years have done: Will you return? Will you refer a friend? What did you like best about your experience today?

Customer referrals are the show-and-tell when it comes to increased customer count. In the age of social media, postings from satisfied customers can reach thousands. Repeat customers will define your core base of loyal customers. This, in turn, will give you the opportunity to turn the referred into loyal zealots. The circular loop will continue, reinforcing itself and sustaining profitability. There will be no need for advertising, marketing, and promotional expenses. Soon, a perfectly executed mission will happen consistently every day because we've narrowed down what's essentially indispensable to your success. Set simple standards to be measured, remain focused, and manage expectations so there are no surprises. When the strength of the correlation is weak, so too will the causation, and the links in the loop need to be examined to see which link needs to be strengthened. To put it differently, if you are not turning a profit, you have to evaluate your food quality, your service, and your decor. The answers will be found in your customer satisfaction score responses. Examine the feedback from your customers, as well as observations from your manager and employees.

Customer decisions about when to dine out are becoming more unpredictable in our changing lifestyle environment. People dine out whenever they feel like it, and operators have to make it seem like they were expecting their customers whenever they arrive.

The chain of added value is completed when it comes to the product. Add to the customers' experience an assortment of "delicious and remarkable food and drinks that meet the highest standards of quality, freshness, and seasonality and combine both modern/ creative and traditional Caribbean styles of cooking." You'll have taken those ingredients you planned for, purchased, received, stored, and issued. You'll have prepped (diced, chopped, and portioned) them; cooked them; and assembled them. And now you'll present to a guest sitting at a table in your dining room the final product. This is your moment of truth internally (or as said in the digital universe, your second moment of truth).

A little bit of academia to add depth to this discourse on customer impressions. A 1993 study by Eugene W. Anderson and Mary W. Sullivan on the antecedents and consequences of customer satisfaction in a utility-oriented framework is worth mentioning here as we examine the trinity of customer satisfaction, repeat business, and financial success. Anderson and Sullivan found that satisfaction is best seen as a function of perceived quality and what they call "disconfirmation," the extent to which perceived quality fails to match expectations. Surprisingly, expectations do not directly affect satisfaction, as is often suggested in literature on satisfaction. In addition, Anderson and Sullivan found that quality that falls short of expectations has a greater impact on satisfaction and repurchase intentions than quality that exceeds expectations. Moreover, they found that disconfirmation is more likely to occur when quality is easy to evaluate. Finally, in terms of systematic variation across firms, they found the elasticity of repurchase intentions with respect to satisfaction to be lower for firms that provide high satisfaction. This implies a long-run reputation effect insulating firms that consistently provide high satisfaction.[4]

Okay, let me rephrase in ordinary parlance. Solutions to challenges are applicable across service industries. And expectation of high quality does not affect satisfaction as much as stated in other literature because, when your restaurant becomes known for providing high quality and high satisfaction, your customers' intent to return is lower than when your restaurant is not known for high quality and satisfaction. In the latter case, when quality exceeds customer expectation, customers' intent to return is higher. This is not to say that, if you are providing high quality and satisfaction, customers will not return. Rather, the point is that surprising your loyal customers with higher quality is a good thing—a strategy that will keep them loyal and not going to the competition. What remains true is that when quality falls short of expectations, this has a greater impact on satisfaction and repurchase intentions than does quality that exceeds expectations.

The debate on the links among customer satisfaction; employee satisfaction (and, thus, loyalty, productivity, safety, commitment, enthusiasm, and retention); and profitability has been overwhelmingly settled by research over the previous two decades.[5] What is now open for dialogue is how much social media and use of digital technology in our data-saturated age has moved the needle from one variable to the next and the impact, if any, on customer impressions.

Until the measurement system is developed, implemented, and analyzed, it's best to continue surveying for yourself. Find out whether your customers were greeted instantly, recognized immediately, and seated fairly by the host. Know whether their food-and-beverage order was taken accurately and delivered in a standard timeframe. Determine whether they were engaged graciously by the server, able to pay for the meal promptly, and invited back politely by the maître d'. Gather feedback appropriately, showing appreciation for the customers' patronage; you can do this all through your walkabout observation in the restaurant and by speaking with employees. Customer service should not be left to chance. You can bet that your employees will perform their best every time. They'll want to meet each service request from customers at various stages and appear to deliver all the customers' requirements just in time.

Developing a team approach to customer service is the tool required to succeed. It opens up channels of communication, allowing team members to seek help where and when it's needed and return the favor when they are asked to assist others. This collaboration eases new employees into the workflow, enabling them to get up to speed without fear of failure. It allows employees time to bond with team members, learn their own strengths and weaknesses, and gain the confidence to propose solutions rather than complain and blame when hurdles arises.

On the other side of the coin, when a team member does not transition smoothly, all the advantages of teamwork—increased productivity, better problem solving, development of new ideas, and the improvement of service standards and customer satisfaction—are lost. And the company's profits decrease. It's up to managers to exercise effective leadership and coaching styles. They must ensure high performers are not punished but, instead, rewarded for their great work and that their leadership style doesn't support low performers' lack of effort, energy, urgency, intensity, and responsibility for meeting the company's standards of service.

Traditionally, the saying in management circles was that employees should be physically present at work and leave personal problems at the door so they can be mentally present as well. That's no longer the case. Building a self-directed, goal-oriented team is how you transform employees into faster, better, and more productive versions of themselves. This is referred to as employee performance optimization. And until employees are able to safely merge their work lives with their "other" lives in a work environment that enables them to relax, joke around, and have fun, you won't achieve it. Only in a supportive environment will employees become energized and more accepting of new ideas, take direction more easily, propose better solutions, and bring their A games every day.

# 5

# FINANCIAL OUTLOOK

Discovering insights from the analysis of data collected, especially in nontraditional areas, brings to the surface new ideas—new ways to improve service delivery or to create or increase new revenue streams. Or, it might at least enable you to get the attention of managers and point them toward emerging trends among your customers.

The traditional bookkeeping models of transaction processing and maintenance, as well as their control functions, have changed. Old standards of big data management and up-to-the-minute financial reporting and management accounting have given way to the development of new measuring yardsticks as performance indicators that compare actual performance to budgeted forecasts.

Now every opportunity with customer contact allows for the collection of data. The more you know about who your customers are; what their occasions for dining are; where they live, work, or visit; and how they heard about you, the better you can personalize their service experience. Everything from reservation to payment and all the stages in between are fair game for collection.

Cashiers' performance when it comes to hospitality has changed. Today's cashier is actively seeking to fill water glasses and breadbaskets, seat guests, turn tables, and fulfill other service requests during peak times when all hands on deck are needed before payment is due. Additionally, cashiers should know how to balance trays in their hands to assist servers in getting drink and food orders to customers "just in time," instead of just being spectators, chatting with colleagues, and getting in the way of servers in the dining room or kitchen. It's challenging enough for servers to be maneuvering between small spaces in a dining room while balancing a tray with drinks in one hand and clearing a path in dining room traffic with the other to avoid an accident. In addition, they have to be sure to give customers the right of way as a courtesy, even patiently waiting for customers to end their conversation with their guest at the table or in the open spaces servers use to go back and forth to the kitchen and bar, all while filling a service request. When the difficulty of this dance is compounded by office employees and managers getting in the way, it deflates and saps servers' energy and desire to serve.

Managers can better utilize their time by knowing exactly at certain stages of dining what stations are busiest so as to lend a hand. Assistance can include any number of simple tasks that support the smooth flow of service, from holding a door to getting a napkin or just asking how they can help. Such an offer goes a long way in earning the servers' respect. Being present and available during busy periods enables a manager to bond with the team and be seen as a leader servers can trust to have their back, rather than someone in the kitchen admiring the chef, overseeing the execution of the precision plating assembly line, or sampling for "food quality."

**Objectives and measures for the financial perspective**

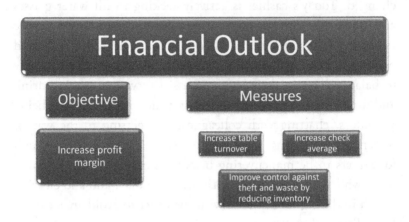

Diagram #6: Financial Outlook Objective and Measures

The overall objective of the financial perspective is to increase sales and profit proportionally. It's important to remember that increased sales does not always equal improved profit. While measuring sales is the most convenient way to measure financial success, in this section, the three measures we'll examine are increasing the average check, reducing waste and spoilage, and increasing the profit margin (see diagram 6). Improved profit is the goal. When we increase the average check, we ultimately increase sales. And, when we reduce waste and spoilage without any increase in the average check and profit margin per menu item, profit will increase in the amount of the reduction in waste and spoilage. Similarly, when waste and spoilage remains the same, along with profit margin per menu item, you can still get an increase in the average check, increase sales, and increase the profit margin as a result of the overall sales mix. There are many pathways to increased profits. Each restaurant must choose a route based on its own unique set of variables or a combination of all available strategies in order to accomplish the goal of increased profits. We will dedicate a section to the measurement of customers, of employees, and of food and beverage items to examine the impact of each on your profitability.

In other words, of all the financial metrics available, we'll look at increasing revenue from last year's target or beating the forecasted revenue projection, whichever is greater. A combination of improving the gross operating profit and controlling variable expenses is still the best ways to measure financial performance. There is no need to go over all the details involved in controlling all the variable line expenses to prove cause and effect. We have a section to answer those concerns. What's important is providing supervision, in the form of standards for purchasing, processes, and procedures, as the ingredients travel through the supply line to production, monitoring each step along the way to the chef's knives and pots. These standards should aim to drive waste and spoilage out of the system. Picking three fundamental indicators to highlight the journey as a path toward achieving the financial goal is the essence of using this approach.

The financial team can then formulate relevant operating targets for each department manager to achieve on a daily basis and for each meal period. Take, for example, the goal of increasing the average check. The dining room manger can collaborate with the chef to acquire knowledge about methods of cooking, use of ingredients, and flavor profile. The manager can then share this knowledge with employees as part of a daily pre-meal meeting for the front-of-the-house team. Servers and managers will then be able to entice the customer palette, helping with purchase selection and suggesting the higher profit margin menu items and beverages; in essence, they will become better salespersons.

Order accuracy, (over) production, portion size, and following recipe specifications are key control points to reducing waste and spoilage. Purchasing ingredients that are in season and have an intended use is pivotal to increasing your company's profit margin. Grow relationships with your vendors. Doing so will give you an external perspective. It's also important to merge your purchases so that you are using the least number of vendors possible and to scale up the volume of your purchases. Both will lead to greater discounts and special purchase offers and, hence, lowering your costs and increasing your profit margin.

In your focus on the financial segment of your business, it's imperative that you work with the data you collected during the customer engagement process. This information will become indispensable, enabling analytical reasoning to be used to propel your operation forward. You'll find new ideas and implement strategies that will continuously improve your operation and delight your customers every time they return. All managers must have year-to-date (YTD) information available at the start of their day, along with nonfinancial information in categories like numbers to indicate the type of comments and complaints that have been received. Comments should be organized according to categories such as food quality, order accuracy, slow service, outstanding performance, inoperative amenities, equipment breakdown, or untidiness. This will allow managers to take an internal temperature reading of the operation's performance. Then their actions can be directed toward making adjustments to the thermostat to get to the ideal temperature in each department. They'll know whether to plan and purchase more or less inventory, to prep more or less ingredients, to produce more or less menu items, and to schedule more or less staff.

It would be remiss to move on to improving the internal cycle without emphasizing the importance of budgets and forecasting. Budgeting and forecasting is a planning exercise for expenses and revenue. It's a tool used as a guide for expected results related to your operation's financial success for a fixed period of time. Referring to this guide and making comparisons with other periods can help you make corrections in order to regain control of the expected results based on future threats and opportunities. Your ability to understand and communicate year-to-date information related to expenses and revenue will not only trigger action, it will also give you depth. In other words, it will help you determine the degree to which you have to make adjustments today for the weeks and months ahead—however long the fixed period of the budget and forecast (the time allotted to get back on track) is in effect. Take, for example, the threat of higher wages as a result of a union agreement or government regulations, on the expense side, while on the opportunity side, a major sporting event is coming to your community. This will prompt increased productivity, in order to gain a reduction in payroll hours and get as close to the previous budget amount as is sustainable without hurting service. Alternatively, you might combine the productivity gains with reduction in other line item expenses, like paper products or cleaning supplies.

Budget and forecast has a cause-and-effect relationship, no different than measures you put in place in other operating areas to achieve a desired outcome. Measures result in an effect on a desired outcome. They are the main drivers of success. To say it differently, applying these measures is like taking your business on a journey in a vehicle replete with a checklist, training manual, and standard operating procedures (SOP) for every individual task. The GPS is your budget and forecast. In the event of a flat tire, you refer to your training manual for tips on how to fix it. The SOP will help you maintain the car in excellent condition and get peak performance by letting you know when to get an oil change or a tune-up, clean the air filters, align your wheels, or check your tire pressure. Proper maintenance will make your journey toward your destination of profitability much more enjoyable. You will use the GPS to avoid threats of accidents; it will guide you to use the best route to avoid traffic. As you pass milestones and directional signs, you will be alerted when to stop for red lights (when you are behind in revenue and over in expenses) and when it's time to make a change in direction. The flashing yellow light comes on, warning that you must proceed with caution (you are ahead in revenue and over in expenses). The green light tells you to continue at full speed (you are ahead in revenue and your expenses are low). At this point, you may have to stop at the gas station to fill up with more employees;

that will rebalance the GPS to ensure revenue and expenses remain in sync to maximize profits.

To conclude, before moving on to improving cycle time, budget and forecasting is subject to the managers' subjective judgment, based on external information (consumer confidence, employment rate, disposable income, gas prices, weather conditions, and the like) and internal information (historic data from the previous weeks, months, and years). The most important key to arriving at objective numbers is to ensure you're comparing apples to apples. For example, be sure that you're comparing last week's Monday to this week's Monday. If January 6, 2015, is a Monday and January 6, 2016, is a Thursday an adjustment must be made for the variance in the day of the week before comparing the two days.

There you have it—training tells you what to do, standard operating procedures say when to do it, and budget and forecasting explain why you're doing it. You'll have measures to identify who your most efficient employee is and what you're most profitable dishes and drinks are. You can rank all your menu items from most to least profitable, and to continue the driving analogy, let this ranking decide which get to continue to be passengers in your car and help you meet more customers. Without this new model car, you are at an increased risk of getting lost and never getting to your destination of sustained profitability.

As we lift up the hood to view and listen to how well our engine is performing figuratively, research aimed at quantifying the links between employee satisfaction and customer satisfaction, productivity and financial performance began in 1980 with Benjamin Schneider's survey of satisfaction levels of bank customers and employees. Let's see where the "rubber meets the road" in our next chapter.

# 6

# IMPROVING CYCLE TIME

Bringing together the competing values of customer impressions and employee satisfaction, in an effort to intensify your customers' experience while they are in your presence, is the heart and soul of the internal cycle. Your organization must adapt and be flexible to change yet stable and controlled for effectiveness.

Here is where discoveries are made in the gap between delivering excellent customer impression and employees' ability to execute. You learn what the needs are for your restaurant—whether that is additional training, upgraded equipment, infusion of technology, or a combination of all three. You'll interweave just enough so as not to overwhelm the user—the customers or employees.

In the case of technology, its availability is not always in sync with widespread usage that includes and is accepted by all age groups. A cautious approach to implementation is best. The desired result is reducing cost, increasing revenue, or simplifying processes and procedures. Often, we mistakenly think only of our customers, when significant savings can be accomplished via productivity gains by employees. Their footprints are equally important and directly related to your restaurant's success. Research—beginning in 1980 with Benjamin Schneider's survey of satisfaction levels of

41

bank customers and employees[6]—has quantified the links between employee satisfaction and customer satisfaction, productivity, and financial performance.

It continued with Frederick Reichheld's *The Loyalty Effect* (1996)[7] and James Heskett, W. Early Sasser, and Leonard Schlesinger's *The Service Profit Chain* (1997).[8] These researchers produced the first sets of hard data quantifying these links. Both studies conclude that there are direct and measurable connections between customer-service variables (such as satisfaction and loyalty), employee variables (satisfaction, enthusiasm, loyalty, commitment, capability, and internal service quality), and financial results.

Further studies by Development Dimensions International, Inc. (DDI), 1997, found evidence of a circular relationship between employee satisfaction and retention, customer satisfaction and loyalty, and increases in company profitability. DDI conducted focus groups, customer interviews, and surveys to determine drivers of an effective service environment. Finally, Dr. Thomas Rollins of the Hay Group developed a model linking employee opinion survey results directly with business performance metrics, while excluding customer satisfaction measures.[9]

The panoramic view of this perspective is to improve operational effectiveness by reducing cycle time. Cycle time starts at the skillful acceptance of a reservation; it moves through your customer being instantly greeted, fairly seated, recognized quickly, and having his or her food-and-beverage order taken accurately and includes timely service and appropriate attainment of feedback, as well as the customer swiftly settling the bill and being graciously appreciated for his or her business and invited to return. Team building, technology, and equipment are the tools to accomplish this goal (see diagram 7).

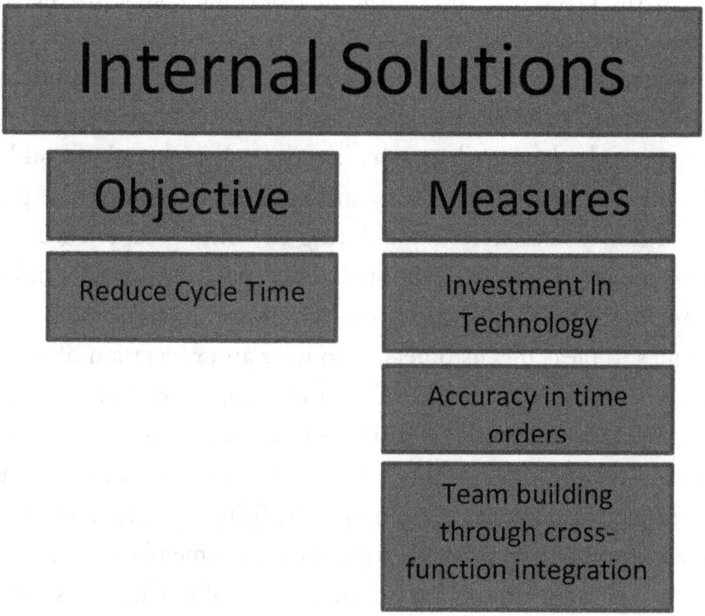

| Internal Solutions | |
|---|---|
| **Objective** | **Measures** |
| Reduce Cycle Time | Investment In Technology |
| | Accuracy in time orders |
| | Team building through cross-function integration |

Diagram #7: Internal Solutions. Objectives and Measures

For starters, let's consider the accuracy of the food and beverage order and the turnaround time to get the plate on the table. After all, these are the primary measures for customer satisfaction in this perspective. If customers have to wait too long or have to ask for their food, then they will go somewhere else where they do not have to wait as long. Leapfrogging your present operating system with the use of technology from, say, pen and paper at point of sale to customer-driven iPads placed at the table are the new order of the day. The goal is, of course, to improve turnaround time and eliminate errors in ordering. What can go wrong when the customer places his or her own order? Change of mind, just guessing. Technology and equipment support an increased turnaround time.

Cohesiveness among the team in the kitchen as they cook and assemble the dish for delivery is their moment of truth.

To the customer, the transition from one course to the next should come just in time. First, establish a standard time for the "I know what I want one item," time-challenged customer. Second, have another standard in place for when multiple courses are ordered, with a time standard for each course. Thirdly, when there is an add-on to a meal ticket, whether an additional person joined the party or additional sales were made during the dining experience, each action must trigger an additional time-sensitive service standard. Come closer for this. Time is too important an issue today when it comes to pleasing customers, who have an expectation of getting what they want now, to leave it to chance. Everything else your customers do today will be available now (i.e., from their handheld device—no waiting necessary). They expect the same from you. Yes, this expectation applies even in upscale, full-service restaurants. Be prepared to be sufficiently staffed, with team members at the right place at the right time based on the amount of touch points needed to deliver timely service.

Each operator will determine what those time standards are, on the basis of his or her type of restaurant, menu, method of cooking, assembly and presentation, employee skill set, equipment, and style of service.

Comparing ideal and actual time for customer-service touch points will become part of your weekly dialogue in management meetings. Use an information management system, one that enables you to record, analyze, and report this data easily.

To measure team building, we will look at the amount of flexibility within the team—the team's ability to carry out more than one function. This measure is important since during busy and peak meal periods it is impossible for a server or cook to handle all the tables of various sizes and stages of dining so that the customer's next service request is fulfilled seemingly just in time. The manager should become aware where and when help is needed by working closely with the servers, bus persons, and culinary staff to achieve this goal.

This team-building effort can be measured by the amount of training hours per employee per month. Measure the effectiveness of each employee within the team and determine the cause-and-effect relationship between training and increasing team and individual productivity. Look at the amount of covers served per hour and per shift and the number of customer complaints, as two examples.

Upgrading equipment to capture savings in space, energy, and convenience can be a good driver. Redesigning workstations so they better match the workflow, streamlining the processes of cooking and assembling dishes, improves the turnaround time.

Once the size of the gap is determined, you can develop a strategic plan to close it, prioritizing your financial goals. Bear in mind that the cost of avoidance until a fix is in place can be used as a teaching moment—to enhance training effectiveness and streamline operational effectiveness under the umbrella of growth, development, and innovation, both internally and externally.

# 7

# GROWTH, DEVELOPMENT, AND INNOVATION

To grow a plant, a person, or an organization, start with a seed. Then collect information and feedback that answers these questions: How am I doing? Where do I want to go? How do I get there? And what do I need to do that?

To transform into a plant, a seed needs soil, accessible water, and the right temperature and light.

Personal growth and development occurs when improvements are made in our physical, emotional, intellectual, spiritual, social, and financial states.

Organizational growth occurs when employees become better versions of themselves, able to accomplish higher performances levels, through the effectiveness of a team.

In the food-service industry, you must get used to the word *change*, as change is constant and considerable. Restaurants must evolve to deal with changing technology, changing customer behavior and expectations, and changing trends. And today, change is occurring at a faster rate than ever before.

Your restaurant has to match the speed of change. Here, when taking on the growth-and-development perspective, is where the mission becomes aligned with the owner's vision, in our example:

- to sell delicious and remarkable food and drinks that meet the highest standards of quality, freshness, and seasonality and combine both modern/creative and traditional Caribbean styles of cooking

- to consistently provide our customers with impeccable service by demonstrating warmth, graciousness, efficiency, knowledge, professionalism, and integrity in our work

- to have every customer who comes through our doors leave impressed and excited to come back again

- to create and maintain a restaurant that is comprehensive and exceptional in its attention to every detail of operation

- to provide all who work with us a friendly, cooperative, and rewarding environment that encourages growth and long-term, satisfying employment

- to keep our concept fresh, exciting, and on the cutting edge of the hospitality-and-entertainment industry

- to be a giving member of the community and to use our restaurant to improve the quality of life in our community

It is worth repeating the mission statement often to reinforce our purpose, as it must guide our actions. Only then will all our actions support our mission. Any action that does not must be abandoned.

Growth, development, and innovation do not occur simultaneously. Depending on what stage in the restaurant life cycle yours happens to be in at this time, one can trigger the other. As an example, if you're not growing, you are in danger of dying. Like a plant lacking water, the right temperature, or sunlight, a restaurant with a deficit in food quality, decor, or service may be on its way out. On the other hand, a solid foundation of the trio in place will trigger sales. Increased sales will provide the resources to grow and reproduce or lead to innovation. In other words, when you remain still and stale when everything around you gets larger and better, you become increasingly irrelevant until you evaporate into thin air. If, however, you get in motion and stay in motion, changing along with the trends, new expectations, and new technology, then you'll feel refreshed, invigorated, and ready to keep going.

Let's return to the plant analogy again. As the tree develops, it will not only grow, it will reproduce, bear fruits, and continue growing. So too will your restaurant. As your roots dig deeper into the community, so will your influence and, hence, ability to increase sales and reproduce at other locations and spread your roots throughout the community.

Continuous learning, nurturing, and innovation will keep individual employees trained beyond their current stations, which in turn will prepare them for leadership roles that will propel the company toward a trajectory of growth and development.

## Objectives and measures of the growth and development perspective

Scientific literature on personal development provides traces of evidence that our beliefs come from doing, not thinking. Therefore, when you train your employees on standard operating procedures—which provide a guideline for obtaining your goals in all segments of the restaurant—be sure the training includes repeatable actions that can be seen and measured. In this way, you can affect changes in behavior and, hence, a cultural shift that will be sustainable in the long term.

When training is continuously reinforced, in tandem with innovation in employee benefits and technology that improves the employee experience, employees' self-esteem will jump through the roof. To put it differently, when you continuously train your employees to reinforce your standard operating procedures in combination with measures such as providing new uniforms, you will observe employees who have a new pride in the job, broader smiles, and a quicker bounce to their steps. Until you set up an employee satisfaction scorecard, with an employee satisfaction survey to measure the bumps, you'll have no way of truly knowing the impact of these measures. Conduct these surveys, and you'll have a quantifiable way, rather than just subjective observation, of understanding the impact training and innovations have—likely better employee attendance and less frequent lateness, a decrease in setup time for service, an increase in coverage per shift, more sales per hour, more tips, and an increase in the average check. There is a big difference between job satisfaction and employee satisfaction and it's impact on your operation. That will be next.

In this segment of your operation is where you evaluate past performance to create new experiences for your customer. The answer is somewhere hidden in all the information previously collected and yet to be organized and analyzed so that an emerging trend jumps out at you to give life to a new service, amenity, or menu item.

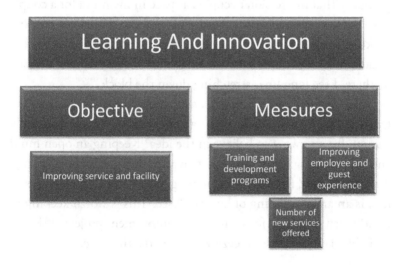

Diagram #8: Learning and Innovation Objective and Measures

As the cliché would have it, "old smells and new sells." That suggests continuously upgrading your restaurant to keep relevant and fresh, keeping up with changing trends and contributing to the customer experience. This is no different from continuously adding and subtracting menu items to delight your customers with current trends and new flavors on their next visit and to ensure they always want to return to see what's new.

Similarly, in architecture, function over form can change to form over function, allowing you to create new ideas on how to fit the form to the function. A few months previous to this writing, I was walking from one appointment to the next on Broadway in the mid-twenties in the Flatiron district. I observed a restaurant that was open but had no signage and not many customers inside. It was lunchtime, so I took the opportunity to quickly grab a bite, guessing I'd arrived before the lunch-hour crush. What I discovered was a perfect example of my suggestion to "create a form to fit function." The salad, soup, and sandwich workstation was plain vanilla flavor, but what blew my mind was the seating area made up of wooden bleachers, similar to seating you'd find at a park or sporting event stadium. That impression occupied a space in my mind for a couple of weeks as I reflected on the creative person who thought of creating parklike seating for a restaurant. It was an ordinary space in the middle of a block turned into a destination. Now every time I pass by there, I see long lines stretching down the block.

*How long did fear of trying that idea cripple the owner's thoughts?* I wondered. Or was the idea originally not communicated forcefully enough for an owner to believe in the idea? Keeping an open mind and being willing to take risks are two attributes of entrepreneurship. The juicy reward from finally squeezing out an innovative, successful idea is an amazing thing of beauty to see. This is worth keeping in mind when resources for a property improvement project (PIP) are available. For sure, the squeeze will be worth the juice.

# 8

# PERFORMANCE MEASUREMENTS

Manage what you measure and inspect what you expect. Make the rounds from the dining room to the kitchen, the storerooms to the loading dock and purchasing office, and the sanitation area to the parking lot, before circling back to your office. Doing this will reduce the amount of fires that so often cripple managers, who must use far too much of their time putting the fires out and are left with less time to implement new initiatives. And it will confirm your belief that a relationship exists between the measures and the goal. The strength of correlation is amplified by seeing it in action. In other words, the data and the observation will be in sync.

Standard operating procedure guidelines play an important role in assisting employees to be their own fire brigade and stop the fire from spreading. They empower employees to create safety and preventive checklists to avoid reoccurrence of fires.

Traditionally, servers were assigned a station in the dining room comprised of a set number of tables for their shift. They maintain the table during service and reset tables with the help of a bus person. At the end of the day, the tables were again set up completely for the next shift, all the side work that accompanied that the particular station was completed, and the server then punched out. A manager would check for completeness when the server punched out and went home and kept mental note of the server's performance as compared to the standard in three categories—"achieved standard," "below standard," or "exceeded standard." Even when you factor in the rolling start time and end time, the server's goal was to do his or her job responsibility and go home. Now with a team approach, when you are finished, you are asked to "help out" your teammates who are still lagging behind. If one table is nursing drinks over conversation and another was a late pickup, it makes sense for servers whose tables were quicker to offer assistance to their colleagues so everyone leaves together.

However, when all else is equal and, in the interest of teamwork and being a team player, a server is asked to offer assistance to a colleague who's clearly responsible for his or her own lag, you've created a situation it's best to avoid. Perhaps the slower teammate needs assistance due to lack of urgency, failing to maintain tables during the meal period, failing to do side work during slow periods of the shift, or chatting in the kitchen and hanging out in the servers' pantry with other employees. Asking the server who constantly had "I've got it" moments to help the deadweight is punishing your star performer for being both mentally and physical present and continuously taking ownership of his or her responsibilities—essentially for doing a great job.

You know who those slackers are, and you let them get away with it. When a team member does not transition smoothly, all the advantages of teamwork—increased productivity, solutions to challenges, new ideas, service standards, and customer satisfaction and increase profits—are lost. It's up to managers to exercise effective supervision, leadership, and coaching style to ensure high performers are not punished for their great work by being required to support low performers' lack of effort, energy, urgency, intensity, and responsibility in meeting the company's standards of service. The longer this person takes to get up to speed, the greater the chances he or she will infect the team and every person he or she works with.

To encourage efficiency in the workplace, adopt as your mantra the cliché "doing more with less." It has exercised my mind recently to separate the more from the less and what we will do with the difference. If it was a just a subtraction—say, four minus two—we would know the answer. But when we want the answer to be one hundred, then there is an inverse relationship between the two terms. The focus here is the use of technology, equipment, and teamwork to broaden the gap between more or less and to quantify the result in numbers.

To quantify the less with numbers, a measure must be established. In the National Basketball Association, players are no longer measured by the amount of points they score, assists, steals, or blocked shots, but by how much time they spend on the floor in an actual game and, in the case of points scored, how many shots were taken to get the points. The measure is called personal efficiency ratings (PER). They measure practice time with each position coach and other soft measures that cannot be quantified. Other examples include compatibility and locker room presence. A similar measure in the military is called the force multiplier capability. When added to and employed by a combat force, force multiplier capability significantly increases the force's combat potential and, thus, enhances the probability of successful mission accomplishment.

We in food service are always playing catch up with business strategies from other industries. Applying these emerging standards always makes us so much better. First, it was SAS Airline's policy, the customer comes first. (Who remembers SAS?) Then it was, oh no, employees comes first, from General Electric. From my earliest recollection of reading business literature during the Jack Welch era, technology came next. Who can argue with that? Following were personal performance measurements to capture behavior of employees that is not financial and can still be measured statistically as they go about the daily routine—punching in, setting up, serving, breaking down, and punching out.

In food service, practice time can be equated with setup, service to an actual game, and locker room presence to breakdown, allowing restaurants to determine a personal productivity rating (PPR) for each employee. Like coaches in the NBA use the information to determine which player to use on offense, which to play on defense or on set plays, food-service managers can now use the information to schedule employees based on meal period and type of service or event. The savings achieved will go to the bottom line or be repurposed to customer-service activities. And just like the NBA, where players are cut, traded, or waived, so too can you fire, transfer, or put on the call list your employees based on their personal efficiency rating when needed.

In the NBA, when teams practice, players are measured in terms of the amount of training time spent with position coaches to see how well the training is transferred to actual performance in game situations. In food-service operations, setup time is the equivalent of practice. During this time, the other department provide us with all the supplies we need to set up the dining room, side stations, and pantry to perform well during actual service. Now we are going to measure the cause-and-effect relationship between the two. How much time is spent setting up and what part of the time was spent getting supplies from other departments, if any, to improve the process? How much time was spent in training for service (the pre-meal meeting is considered a training session)? These actions must be measured, even if it takes a person with a stopwatch following an employee around his or her daily routine to establish a baseline standard for particular set tasks or for a team to gather supplies and set up the dining room. This can then be compared to having the departments deliver to the dining room to determine which model is more efficient. Service measures can be attained by examining servers' covers per hour/shift, average checks, total sales, percentage of tips, and beverage sales. All these variables are slices of the sales pie that will be compared to the whole pie and to other servers on the shift. This will show how each server ranked in terms of all the variables individually, as well as totally, giving him or her a personal performance rating (PPR) or index.

In the culinary department, measure preparation time for any applicable tasks, from deboning a whole chicken to prepping a filet mignon or a rack of lamb or even a bag of carrots to *mise en place*. Measure also turnaround time for an order ticket and establish a benchmark time—a standard by which other employees' performance of the same task will be compared. This will enable the chef to schedule his or her team to match not only the skill set needed for the menu and covers expected but also the efficiency needed for proper execution of both speed and accuracy in preparing menu dishes. Take into account the turnaround time for pots and pans, small utensils, cutting boards, and trays for culinary; glassware for the bar; tableware for dining room; props for holding, heating, and presenting; and serving equipment, as well as glassware, flatware, and silverware for catering special events. Maintenance, delivery, shrinkage, cost, and usage are the key variables when it comes to developing metrics for the kitchen manager or chief steward.

Purchasing will have its own unique variables based on how well it plans, purchases, receives, stores, and issues ingredients for production to the chef. So too will you measure maintenance, labeling, cleanliness, and ease of finding things across all storerooms dry and cold with your eyes closed. A good test is to see whether, when power is interrupted, business continues as usual.

The human resources department will be judged by its ability to attract, screen, select, and orient candidates—delivering new hires to their designated departments for further orientation and training by an assigned trainer. The new hire will then pass a skill observation assessment and be entered into a training and development database. This database will be used to develop more training, enabling new hires to gain confidence, grow, and feel empowered. This will ensure that their intrinsic qualities benefit the restaurant and the customer.

Turnover, retention, job satisfaction, and employee satisfaction are key metrics. Once these metrics are established, especially the personal performance ratings, you will not be able to differentiate between the Anthonys and Marys and Sallys among your employees.

Until then, those differences will remain as wide as the Pacific Ocean, and the similarities as narrow as a pinhead. Your Anthonys and Marys will be friendly and engaging and always busy, their uniforms clean and crisp. Sally, on the other hand, will start one task, say getting the forks ready for the place settings, and then she will stop to chat with one team member and then another—you know, engaging in small talk about last evening, the kids, and on and on as the team members try their best not to ignore her while continuing their setup. She'll then switch to spoons and then glasses, while picking on another team member, trying to get into his or her business. When the managers walk in to check on the progress of the setup, Sally will jump to attention, focusing on whatever items she has in her hand so as to appear part of the team setting up the room for service. As soon as the manager leaves, she'll go to the mirror to fix her hair, put on her makeup, and adjust her uniform. Then she'll sit down to fold napkins with those who completed the setup. Meanwhile, Anthony will be busy making sure the team has enough supplies for setup, stocking the side stations and coffee service, and ensuring all the little details are in place so the team will be ready for service.

During service, Anthony will constantly offer everyone help when he is not busy with his tables so service can flow smoothly. Sally, on the other hand, will use the bus person as her surrogate to do her job, and when it's a busy night, she'll ask for an "early out" to avoid the breakdown, reset, and cleanup activities.

Personal performance rating is the solution to the Sallys of the restaurant world. Productivity, not activity, is the measure of personal performance. PPR's serve as an early warning system. To compound this unhappy situation, all else equal, the low performer completes the same work in longer hours and will, therefore, earn more wages than the high performer in the traditional arrangement. So in two ways, the high performers are punished, rather than rewarded, receiving less pay and doing more work. If the situation is allowed to continue, the high performers will be demoralized, and sooner rather than later, they will sink to the level of the misfits. Like a hurricane that causes massive damages in low-lying areas in its path, low performers will damage the productivity of an organizational structure you depend on to deliver high quality performance. And it can take a long time to rebuild.

Effective supervision, wise leadership styles, and one-on-one coaching can help change behavior, enabling low-performing employees to become better team members. Give these employees a timeframe in which to demonstrate their ability to meet a new performance standard. Or you might give them stand-alone assignments, such as positioning them at a carving station, where the damage can be minimized. You might even schedule them at the end of a list, using them only on a limited basis, when you just need bodies present or when all else fails terminate.

Low performers are always very chatty, friendly, and engaging with other employees. They're interested in their colleagues' personal business. And then they play hide-and-seek with supervisors, attempting to appear ever busy when in the supervisors' presence. These workers appear to have attention deficit disorder, unable to focus on one task and see it through to completion. Rather, they assist others completing tasks nearby, seeking praise for its completion. These outliers can skew employee satisfaction survey results because, yes, they are satisfied with getting a paycheck and benefits. However, they're not satisfied with being held accountable for fulfilling their assigned job description.

Accounting and bookkeeping are all about numbers. They're about providing analytical data, both financial and operational, in a useful format that will aid in making decisions and judgment calls and taking action based on each department's targeted goals. Measuring the accounting department has to do with variables that improve the data-collection process, ensuring it's in sync with department solutions. In other words, you should not be playing jeopardy with your data, collecting solutions only when you encounter a problem. Rather, you should know both the questions and answers ahead of time—information you'll gain by searching the data collected. Although you may accidentally discover a solution to an existing problem while dicing and chopping around the data, usually the data will lead you to things you do not know, and learning will be a process of discovery.

The current trend is to become more analytical as profit margins are squeezed thin due to increased cost of ingredients, labor, and utilities. To offset these increases, it becomes necessary to find ways to operate more efficiently. A point of sales system (POS) is a great tool for maintaining up-to-the-minute information on what's happening in your restaurant, at any time of the day. The aggregate is already chopped to a fine dice (excuse the pun) to give you a picture, in real time, of the state of your operation. Again, this information can be used to take action, make judgment calls, and decide on a course of action for the remainder of the day—all ensuring you get your desired result. With the use of social media today, changes can be made instantly to your menu, offering for a "day part" to improve sales expectations.

If you are not actively using the information collected, then your POS is just a cosmetic addition to your operation. Ideally, additional software can be tied into your POS. For example, ChefTec's complete inventory system enables you to reduce time spent on purchasing and ordering by up to five times. In today's economy, it is vital for food-service operations to find ways to save time and money while reducing back-of-the-house processes.[10] You can now use technology to measure productivity from point of purchased ingredients to point of sale and everything in between.

Key performance indicators will be defined as those you do not get on your POS. We do use the aggregate to perform further statistical analysis—a higher order of thinking, reasoning, and inference—as we take a deep dive into the numbers.

Let's take a look at the available measures you can choose from like a buffet. In some instances, where there is no quantifiable data, we suggest you do a time-and-motion study to arrive at a hard number that can be utilized for further analysis with known data. To remain focused on the critical areas of measurement not found on a POS, we will do what tailors do best—measure twice and cut once. Keep focusing on the target, not on firing scattered shots, hoping to hit the target. Attendance, training, and performances (ATP) are critical additional measures we will focus on. Here's a list of those available measures:

## Cost of Food Sold

Opening Inventory + Purchases – Closing Inventory = Cost of Food Sold

## Food Cost

Requisition + Transfers In – Transfers Out = Food Cost (for whatever interval you are measuring)

## Average Inventory

Opening Inventory + Closing Inventory/2 = Average Inventory

## Inventory Turnover Rate

Cost of Food Sold/Average Inventory = Inventory Turnover Rate

**Menu Mix Percentage**

Number of Items Sold / Total Number of All Items Sold

**Menu Mix Percentage Popularity Rate**

100 / number of menu items x 70%

**Popularity Factor**

Item Popularity Index / Item Expected Popularity

**Expected Equal Popularity Factor**

1 / the number of items in the group

**Menu Item Contribution Margin**

Item Selling Price – Item Food Cost

**Total Items Contribution Margin**

Number of Items Sold × Item Contribution Margin

**Total Item Revenue**

Number of Items Sold × Menu Price

**Total Item Food Cost**

Number of Items Sold × Item Food Cost

**Total Menu Contribution Margin**

Total Menu Revenue – Total Food Cost

## Average Contribution Margin

Total Item Contribution Margin / Total Number of Items Sold

## Personal Efficiency Ratings

Assume X = the standard time for one person to set up dining room. In this sample, we'll say forty-five minutes is our standard time (x = 45 minutes). When you schedule three persons, then, your expectation is that setup will take fifteen minutes. This is a simple standard set, measured from a time-and-motion study. Now, you can schedule based on a standard. No more guesstimating. This is one part of the equation for personal performance measurements of all the various tasks a server does during the course of his or her shift. At the end of a shift, you take the reading from the POS.

Total covers (A) = 180; Total hours (B) = 12; Total Sales (C) = $10,000; Total Tips (D) = $1,600;

Number of servers (E) = 3; Average Sales per hour (F) = 833.33; Average cover per hour (G) = 15;

Average check (H) = $55.56; tip percentage of sales (I) = 16%; average tip percentage (J) = (6.67%);

## Server A Server B Server C

Sales $3,675 $4,025 $2,300

Covers 55 90 35

Tips $590 $ 760 $250

Hours 4 5 3

|  | Server A | Server B | Server C |
|---|---|---|---|
| PER Score: Sales | .37 | .40 | .23 |
| PER Score: Covers | .31 | .5 | .19 |
| PER Score: Tips | .37 | .48 | .16 |
| PER Score: Hours | .33 | .42 | .25 |
| Total PER Score | 2.8 | 2.7 | .88 |
|  |  |  |  |

Diagram #9: Four variable measures

### Personal Efficiency Ratings

| Weight | Variable | Total | Server A | Server B | Server C |
|---|---|---|---|---|---|
| 25 | Sales | 1500 | 85 | 860 | 555 |
| 25 | Covers | 25 | 4 | 12 | 9 |
| 25 | Hours | 14 | 2 | 6 | 6 |
| 25 | Tips | 308.5 | 25.5 | 172 | 111 |
|  |  |  |  |  |  |
|  | Sales Score |  | 1.4 | 14.3 | 9.3 |
|  | Covers Score |  | 4.0 | 12.0 | 9.0 |
|  | Hours Score |  | 3.6 | 10.7 | 10.7 |
|  | Tips Score |  | 2.1 | 13.9 | 9.0 |
|  | Total PER |  | 23.6 | 73.9 | 63.4 |
|  |  |  |  |  |  |
|  |  |  |  |  |  |
|  | Sales Per Cover | 60 | 21.25 | 71.666667 | 61.66667 |
|  | Covers Per Hour | 1.785714 | 2 | 2 | 1.5 |
|  | Tip Rate | 0.205667 | 0.3 | 0.2 | 0.2 |

Diagram #10: Personal Efficiency Ratings

In diagram 9 above, we use four variables with equal weights of 25 percent to get a personal efficiency rating (PER) for the top three servers. The same can be done for attendance, punctuality, absences, setup and breakdown, reset, or any number of other variables that are critical to your success. The weighted value would change based on the number of variables used.

To get the percent of employees trained within fourteen days, use this formula:

Divide the total number of employees trained in fourteen days by the total number of employees eligible for training and multiply by 100

(Total no. employees trained in 14 days) / (Total no. employees eligible for training) × 100

Employees must be trained by a designated department trainer and must pass a skill observation assessment and be entered into the training and development database for employees

- The fourteen-day window begins at the employee's hire date and ends fourteen days later.

To get the employee staffing percent, use the following:

- Divide the total number of active employees by the total target number of employees and multiplying by 100.

(Total no. active employees) / (Total no. employee staffing target)x 100

A full scope of performance measurements in restaurants can be endless. The key is selecting those that are critical to your success and those that can give you early warnings, enabling you to avoid any hurdles that might emerge.

# 9

# EARLY WARNING SYSTEM

According to *Wikipedia*, predicative analysis "encompasses a variety of statistical techniques from predictive modeling, machine learning, and data mining that analyze current and historical facts to make predictions about future or otherwise unknown events."[11]

Predictive analytics is used in actuarial science, marketing, financial services, insurance, retail, travel, and health care. And now, it's useful in food service as well. We will unitize data collected on customers' footprints to harness the analytical outcome into information that, when used wisely, will improve every area of restaurant operations, reduce failure rate, and give operators a better work-life balance while at the same time improving the customer and employee experience. It will become our early warning system.

*Predicative analysis* and *emotional intelligence* are becoming the new buzzwords related to the use of technology and people to attract and retain customers and improve their service experience. In consumer product industries and financial services, these principles have been applied over a longer period of time, and results have been accumulated, analyzed, and utilized to improve company performance. In food service, the information is used to create new menu items and make special occasion food events better. These concepts enable you to be aware of anniversary dates so that you can invite customers to return for such occasions that make customers feel valued and special. And they give you the opportunity to increase repeat visits, enormously improving resell, upsell, and cross-sell rates. Consider a year and the number of occasions on which one customer dines out, other than need. Each year contains personal events, such as birthdays, family reunions, weddings, date night, girls' night out, business-retirement parties, training workshops, Christmas parties, and incentive and recognition dinners. Multiply that by each member of the household.

We begin the process of collecting information skillfully with reservation. It's important to prioritize capturing the caller's telephone number and e-mail address. You'll also want to find out why the customer will be dining out. Reasons may range from the functional, such as "doesn't feel like cooking" or "craving a particular dish" to the experimental—for example, "want to try a new restaurant" or "want to try a new cuisine." Or perhaps the customer will be celebrating a special occasion. Be sure the information is coded. It then becomes data.

In some cases, the words *information* and *data* are intertwined. Some say you collect data, and then it became information. I believe it's information first, and then it turns into data before it becomes knowledge that can be used wisely.

However you think of the information-data flow, it's important to continue assembling data. Collect information on menu item choices, categorized as appetizers, main courses, and desserts, as well as beverages, broken down into categories like wine, beer, spirits, champagne, liqueur, and specialty coffees. Then complete your data collection with a customer survey incorporated into the payment receipt. This will allow you to gather information on how, when, and why the customer used your service by offering a reward for completion of the survey.

Now you have a rich source of data to be refined and then turned into knowledge by slicing, dicing, and smashing the data into small bites of wisdom that you can apply to the customer's next visit. Or use what you've learned to entice customers back with a specific offer that customizes their previous purchasing behavior. Remember that the customer's footprint can be sliced into four pieces that mirror the four operational segments of your restaurant. Customer impressions match the moment of truth contact point; food and beverage choices reflect the internal cycle; payment is a replica of your financial outlook; and the invitation to return is parallel to your learning and innovation segment.

With this stack of data, you want to act like an air traffic controller with jurisdiction over a designated airspace of your own. There, you can scan the data, looking for changing conditions from four directions—customer impressions; financial outlook; internal cycle; and growth, development, and innovation. With this 360-degree panoramic view, your role is twofold. First, you must identify threats and opportunities by scanning the data and passing it on to those flying below the radar, in this case your managers. This information will enable them to make correction to their course of action to avoid (a) near misses and (b) head-on accidents or to proceed (c) with cautions or (d) full-speed ahead. Secondly, for restaurants flying at higher altitudes, you want to capture what is trending in menus, service style, customer behavior, social media usage, equipment, and community events. You will also pass this information on to managers, who will translate it and make judgment calls based on its potential impact, if any, to improve the operation of each department.

A near miss related to customer impression might be a customer complaint about the steak being undercooked, where the server made the recovery immediately and the customer left completely satisfied and proved it with return visits. Your server now has the knowledge that his or her actions kept this customer loyal. A head-on accident might look something like your average check and sales declining along with your customer satisfaction scores. Certainly red light alerts from your financial outlook will tell you where you have to stop and change direction. Place heavy emphasis on customer-service training, salesmanship, food quality, and customer engagements to clear a new path.

A good example of when you'll want to proceed with caution is when your internal cycle reports sales are rising and cost of goods and/or labor costs are declining. Inspect your purchasing, portion control, and production processes and procedures to determine that your standards are being maintained and the savings truly are a result of lower costs of ingredients purchased or whether they're only seasonal. Check to see if the lower labor cost is the result of training to simplify the process of serving and increase servers' efficiency and, thus, ability to serve more customers per hour or per shift, whichever measure you use, resulting in reduced labor hours.

Adversely there is always a lag in results when the chef and dining room manager, in the quest to gain bonuses by hitting certain targets in food and labor costs, cut back in terms of quality and quantity of ingredients purchased and fewer food servers scheduled. This creates stressful circumstances for servers. It's a case of dining room managers taking advantage of a situation in which the effects are felt after the period under review—the period for which they'll have receive their reward.

What is so notable about the early warning system, which is one component of a balanced approach to managing your restaurant, is that each action has a cause-and-effect reaction. And the reaction doesn't just take place within a specific department. Rather, it ripples through all the restaurant's interdependent departments. The strength of the causes and effects must we weighted to bring attention to what they are and where they become joined at the hip. This management model helps you to identify what is critical to the success of your restaurant, and knowing the cause and effect enables you to amplify the causes in order to accelerate positive effects and vice versa.

# DEPARTMENT SCORECARDS

### Dining room scorecard

Externally, everyone seems to be tuned in to his or her device for work, shopping, and to seek places to go. Now more than ever restaurants have to compete in that crucial space on social media in order to get customers' attention, whet their appetites, and earn their dollars. You have to create emotional and sensory experiences so customers will want to spend time at your restaurant.

Once you've drawn customers in, gaining their physical presence, loop back to social media. For in this era, social media is the new word-of-mouth advertising. If your restaurant's sensory stimulation is not sufficient to delight the palette or its ambiance fails to transport customers to another place, the background music setting the mood for relaxation, people won't talk about your restaurant online. If your employees have no personality to share, there is no communal space, or the Wi-Fi connection is insufficient, then next time customers will just sit at their computer in the office or at home with a book and order online delivery. After all, why else would they come to your restaurant but for the social element?

To say it differently, you have to make your restaurant the cool spot to be. Tech savvy, high energy, or laid back, allow for things like fun pairing of food and beverage with other activities that appeal to your customers. Be sure that nothing appears corporate or stuffy (for example, comments like "Let me check with my manager"). Create a burst of emotions—the wow factor is the new way of building loyalty building for now and for the future. Expanding the meaning of hospitality and how food and beverage fits into the mix with customer behavior and lifestyle can only enhance the experience. Internally, this equates with three of your mission points:

- to sell delicious and remarkable food and drinks that meet the highest standards of quality, freshness, and seasonality and combine both modern/creative and traditional Caribbean styles of cooking

- to consistently provide our customers with impeccable service by demonstrating warmth, graciousness, efficiency, knowledge, professionalism and integrity in our work

- to have every customer who comes through our doors leave impressed and excited to come back again

With all that is written about customer and employee satisfaction and which is more important, as well as the trifecta of quality food, extraordinary decor, and excellent service (and how each contributes to customer retention, loyalty, and by extension financial success), studying these points can be overwhelming. How often is it written that none of this can be accomplished without the first step— employees showing up to work as scheduled and on time? Rarely. However, if this doesn't settle the debate on who is more important, then nothing else will. And by the same token, extraordinary decor and insanely delicious food also contribute to employee retention and loyalty, just like they do for customers. The key to sustained success, then, is the employer providing the same excellent service to employees they expect customers to receive. When there is a fracture in this circular loop, every effort must be made to strengthen the realignment.

So the earliest warning system for a food-service operation failure is the owner or manager's mind-set. When he or she thinks first of himself or herself and then that customers come first, disaster may be impending. Every successful and savvy operator knows that it's not about him or her but, rather, the employees and then the customers, which equates to good service experience, mouthwatering food, and profitability. Diagram 10 below indicates the various measures to choose from the four operating segments to be successful.

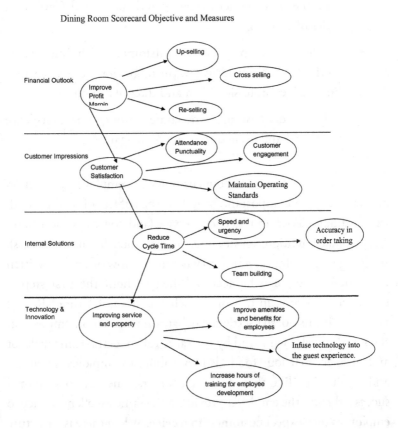

Diagram #11: Dining Room Scorecard Objective and Measures

**Example of a Dining Room Scorecard**

As we move forward—using a balanced approach to seamlessly align the owner's mission statement with first the restaurant's departments and then the actions of the employees—remember that it's been possible thanks to a clear vision and a broad mission that every employee can rally around.

In this section, we're going to put those words into a plan of action and behavior.

What distinguishes your restaurant from those of the competitors? Your employees and your customers. The more you get to know your customer, the better you will be able to personalize their service needs. In addition to the great food and ambiance they already love and enjoy, your employees must understand clearly that there is value added in the style of service and engagement with the customers. This is the key to long-term prosperity. To put it differently, when you combine delicious food and a wow ambiance with wiggle room for employee engagement with your customers, you'll creates a "force multiplier effect," enabling you to better accomplish the mission of customer satisfaction. The more this effect takes hold of your customers, the more they'll want to come back, tell more friends, and purchase more food and drinks.

Restaurant work is labor intensive. What other industry takes raw ingredients and turns them into a finished product, ready to consume—all from an order received from a customer waiting at a table in a dining room? It's a recipe for instant gratification or deflated expectation. No shelf life, no recall notice before it gets in the stomach, and the brain is delighted. It's game, set, match point all wrapped in one. The customer can walk in at any time feeling hungry and expect to be served as if he or she was expected and just in time to get back to the office for a meeting. There is no algorithm to predict that behavior. The entire industry is based on this unpredictable behavior; it is, in fact, what restaurants thrive on—to make the impossible happens. It's your employees who must have thick, smooth skin in order to be calm and make it happen.

This is where emotional intelligence comes in to play. Restaurant employees must be able to decipher whether the couple who just got seated in their station is on a first date, a business meeting, or celebrating an anniversary. They must be able to hold their emotions in check when a party of eight leaves an insufficient tip or none at all, not allowing the slight to affect their smile and service at the next table. Will their confidence remain? Will they be able to fall back on their great qualities, such as resiliency and self-motivation, and still deliver the service experience you expect? Will they know how to pay attention to their customers and not be distracted by the small talk between other employees that often occurs during service? And, more importantly, can they hold off leaving the floor to use personal devices?

The last hurdle is the artistic work of the chef. A chef's art is expressed in his or her choice of ingredients, combined with his or her skill with a knife and eye for aesthetics. A chef must prepare food with the right amount of heat; be able to interweave texture, colors, flavors, and shapes; and create an arrangement on a porcelain dish that contrasts in shape, size, and color designed to intensify the arousal of the palate.

Can you see now how important the responsibility of the person delivering is? Can you see how important training is to your employees? They are carrying the hopes and inspiration of the chef. They are transporting the expectation of the girls' night out to have fun. They are carrying the vision of the owner. It can never be left to chance. Training, more training, and continuous training is the answer. Considering the enormous responsibility your employees carry, the onus to make it happen is on you the operator. Take the time to screen carefully and select wisely, and your investment in training will pay dividends. Each employee comes with an expectation to be trained regardless of his or her previous experience. Do it. Do not let an employee's previous experience leak into your operation. You have invested too much time and money to set up processes and procedures that will guide your employees' every step along the way. Everyone will be trained and held accountable as part of a team to perform individual tasks in each department—be that to purchase, to receive, to store, to prep, to cook, to assemble, to pick up, to serve, or to clean. Make your training simple, easy to follow, and difficult to do wrong.

Let me share this story that captures the essence of how lack of training or process and procedures, the resulting employee behavior, and the interconnection among all departments affects customer service. This is a true story—one you couldn't make up even with the most creative imagination. Here's some background to set the stage for this fantastic drama play. Imagine this—an employees' dining room, the fringe benefit of a large financial service firm in the Wall Street area. It subsidizes menu prices to make staying in the building to dine an attractive option; is open for breakfast, lunch, and dinner; and serves over five thousand meals a day. The dining room is full of action stations and self-serve stations and offers a wide variety of ethnic cuisines to match the diversity of employees.

I was filling in temporarily for a receiving clerk. The opportunity to observe and listen to what I like to call the engine room of food service—the kitchen—was priceless. The kitchen was very large, with an equally large service team. My day started early, at 6:00 a.m., with pallets of fruits, vegetables, dairy, meats, and dry goods to greet me on arrival. The manager was already busy going through the pallets, verifying the accuracy of the order and comparing the goods with the delivery invoices. My task was to begin the storing process in the various storage areas, refrigerators, and freezers nearby. A simple and easy task—until the brigade of cooks looking for their ingredients to begin prepping to meet their production quota for the day intersected. The cooks reminded me of taxi drivers in the city searching for a fare who, spotting a hand in the air, will cut off other drivers, in a race to pick up the passenger. The cooks, similarly, picked off the ingredients from the pallets before they'd been counted or as they were on their way to storage. In the former instance, I had to chase them down to note where their station was so I could later verify the missing amount.

I continued to observe and to listen to the engine revving up on all cylinders. I took in the sound of knives slicing through crisp fresh fruits and vegetables; the colorful language used to communicate with varied accents; the swift and measured steps, seemingly budgeted to keep close to the target work stations; and the musical sounds of pots and pans clanging, reminding me of the steel bands of my native country. All of this added to the potpourri of sights and sounds.

On completion of my primary duties, I was assigned to whichever station needed the most help to make the eleven o'clock deadline for lunch service. One day, my assignment was to assist the pot washer. He was overwhelmed with pots and pans like I had never seen before for one person. His was a spacious workstation, hidden away in one corner of the floor, with a nice view. Even with adequate shelf racks and loading table space for the incoming traffic of pots and pans, we could barely keep up to match the demand for their return use.

Then, when other areas were overrun with orders, during the peak lunch period, it was me pinch-hitting, to use a baseball analogy, to keep the frontline stocked. Soon, the cooks were complaining about running out of pots and pan. You guessed it, I was reassigned to the pot-washing station.

This time, I was quite surprised when I arrived at the pot washer's station, only to find that he'd apparently caught up. I assumed that the traffic of dirty pots must have slowed down significantly, sufficiently to allow one person to wash all those pots I'd observed when previously at the station—when pots with burnt food at the bottom and baked-on stains were being delivered left and right. Hot pots just off the stove had been arriving without warning. So I was impressed.

The pot washer was additionally responsible for taking the trash out, and it was time to make a trip. I was left alone; no problem.

As the cooks began circling, seeking out clean pots and pans, I sensed something amiss. Yes indeed, those large, hard-to-clean pots and pans that required extra effort and strength to remove the stains, burnt and buried at the bottom, had gone out with the garbage. The pot washer confessed this to me later on when another hot pot was delivered without warning.

Pot washing was clearly the least desirable task, to be performed by the lowest rung on the food-service ladder, in isolation. Yet everyone up the service chain ladder depended on this task. Given this fact, why was he treated this way? The kitchen area to which he was assigned was deficient. He was isolated, unable to feel like a part of the team. He was treated without courtesy, hot pots or pans coming his way without warning. The cooks expressed no empathy or understanding and seemed insensitive to his situation, worrying only about the fact that they needed those pots and pans returned clean and sanitized. This lack of empathy is directly related to the fact that the pot washer was performing his task in isolation; the others had no direct view of the volume of dishes he was tasked with cleaning. This was clear from the attitude of the cooks, which was expressed in how they left the pots and pans. They were in the best position to assist in removing some, if not all, of the burnt and caked-on scraps of food. In addition, communicating and prioritizing which pots and pans would be needed first, instead of just dumping them all on him, would have alleviated some of the stress and sense of being overwhelmed that the pot washer faced.

Organizing the stewarding department for success is next.

## Stewarding scorecard

The vision of the owner—to create and maintain a restaurant that is comprehensive and exceptional in its attention to every detail of operation—resonates to all departments. This is especially true of stewarding, where maintenance, sanitation, and cleanliness are the primary mission and employees are handling tableware, pots, pans, utensils, and small equipment.

This department must focus on one area of the mission:

- to provide all who work with the restaurant a friendly, cooperative, and rewarding environment that encourages growth and long-term, satisfying employment

If in the story we shared earlier, the restaurant's environment encouraged growth and satisfaction, two major issues would have been prevented. The pot washer would not have throw out the dirtiest pots and pans with the garbage, because the cooks' attitudes would have been different and they wouldn't have left large amounts of burnt scraps of food in the hot pots or delivered them without warning and communication.

When you discover issues such as these, training and continuous training will eventually change the mind-set of your employees, enabling them to function cooperatively as a team, be emphatic with one another, and always consider your guests' total experience first in every action they take.

Tableware, like any product or service, is vulnerable to improper handling—in this case, both before and during the dishwashing process. Therefore, your tableware investment truly is in the hands of your servers, busboys, dishwashers, and washing machines. By training your staff to follow important steps, you will maximize your tableware investment and increase your bottom line with less breakage.

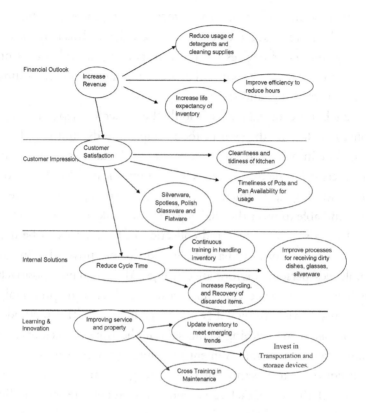

Diagram #12: Department Scorecard

## Example of a Stewarding Scorecard

The key to maximization of the tableware investment is training—never an overused word in food service. All staff and personnel who come into contact with the tableware must be taught proper handling techniques. Always give steward department team members incentives for low breakage records each month, in addition to offering positive reinforcements to other complementary department personnel who handle tableware. Keep a mental and/or written record of accidents and who was responsible. This will help you identify the biggest loser of tableware on your team. Such observation can then be analyzed to improve processes and procedures that will reduce breakages caused by preventable accidents. This may include purchasing better devices for the transporting of tableware from the source of usage to sanitation for scraping, stacking, loading, washing, catching, and storing.

Each type of tableware should be collected separately and containers for the disposal of food scraps, liquids, and recyclables should be in place and easily accessible. In the latter case, the team members from the dining room will communicate with those from the stewarding department to be sure the two departments are in sync and able to meet the challenges of the peak times of service.

Records of breakages and collection of breakages can be used as a" floating record" and as visible evidence incentives that impact employees' personal performance ratings. Also when used positively, such visible evidence can show how the absence of preventable accidents impacts profitability and wage increases. This method— as compared to anything being said at the time of accidents—is more likely to net improvement in employees' tableware handling techniques. Pictorials showing tableware, glassware, and silverware, along with the cost of each can reinforce the proper care and handling of these items and help eliminate preventable accidents. Diagram 11 is your road map to success in stewarding and must be customized to your objectives and unique situations.

Not only is clean noticeable, it really is a valuable investment. How spotless your tableware dishes are, how burnished your silverware shine, and how well your glassware glows and sparkles leaves a lasting impression on customers and impacts the likelihood of their returning. It's not just what customers eat, but what they see, smell, and feel that decides whether or not they want to dine with you again. A great clean involves not just your dish machine, but also the right dose of chemicals and sanitizers, dispensing equipment, temperature, and proper rack loading.

Here are some tips to improve your tableware handling and cleaning operation.

- Know your water. Your water source can cause problems you aren't aware of, such as higher energy costs, operational issues, and inferior cleaning results.

- The right chemicals can save you money and reduce cost. Use cleaning chemicals that get your dishes clean the first time.

- Don't overload and blame the machine. You may be putting more dishes through per rack than the machine is designed to handle. Overloading your machine can reduce the machine's ability to clean and will lead to more rework if the dishes aren't clean.

- Lime scale wastes energy. As your dish machine creates lime scale, it uses more energy to hold the right temperature and takes longer to dry dishes, both of which increase your energy bills.

- Enforce cleaning and disinfecting protocols. Train employees to clean and disinfect, particularly when dealing with the removal of difficult soils. Always adhere to the board of health recommendations for temperature and sanitizer usage to prevent microorganism contamination.

- Buildup can damage your machine. Your machine cleans less effectively with lime scale buildup. Lime scale buildup can cause nozzles to clog, leading to costly labor to delime and remove microbial growth.

- Demand high-quality service. Quality service and regular preventive maintenance programs are keys to successful a dishwashing operation.

- Separate dishes by size

- Pre-rinse.

Culinary Scorecard Objective and Measures

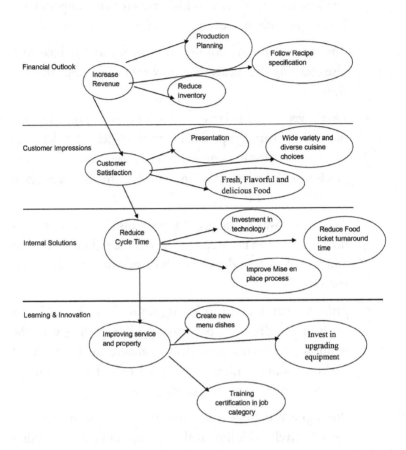

Diagram #13: Department Scorecard Objective and measures

## Culinary scorecard

The kitchen is where unseen value is added. Here ingredients are transformed into delectable menu items. And it's all thanks to schedules, production details, policies and processes, cooking styles and methods; these details are where restaurants live and die. A continuous commitment to service and craft and to preserving the professional image of the chef is imperative.

The heat of the kitchen, contrasted with the calm creativity of a chef whipping up his or her brigade of cooks to produce insanely delicious food presented like a piece of museum art on a porcelain canvas is a thing of beauty. I'm a fan of chefs worldwide. That being said, the main entrée of any menu is the focal point of the dining experience. The pressure to execute with perfect precision in both preparation and presentation of the dish every time is equivalent to that of a golfer trying to hit a hole in one on every shot on the course. All the preparation and perspiration before the food ticket comes up in the kitchen is what we want to measure to ensure efficiency is maximized and the best ingredients are used.

The translation of the bigger picture of the owner's vision and mission to the culinary team is what we will focus on in this section. Diagram 12 above is your visual blueprint.

In the culinary arena, much like in the dining room, conflict and stress are the highest in times of change. Both can be reduced when change is guided by the translation of the owner's vision into the mission and when resources are marshaled for their most efficient and effective use based on the highest priority goal. So, for example, when the goal is to offer the highest standard and quality of ingredients, in terms of freshness and seasonality, in order to sell delicious and remarkable food and drinks, the chef's decisions and judgments should drive the purchasing decisions, within some financial parameters of course. This means communicating how important it is that ingredients be the freshest, perhaps via a rallying call to vendors from the purchasing manager and the receiving clerk being clear that a great sardine is always better than a lobster that does not meet the chef's specification.

Use pictorials, diagrams, checklists, and signage to communicate critical success points of time and temperature, cleanliness and tidiness, preparation and speed, and precision and accuracy. This will keep everyone who comes into the kitchen to perform the daily routine on the same page as the chef.

Offer continuous training to improve the knife skills of the culinary team members and help them achieve certification in their job category. This will be good preparation for the next step forward in growth and development. Although there may not be opportunities for all to jump into, at least your culinary employees will stay motivated and satisfied with their present situation, which will in turn enable them to produce remarkable food.

Keep up with changing dining trends and customer likes. Introduce new dishes to pique the interest of your loyal customers, who'll return to see what's new, expand their cuisine knowledge, and stay on the cutting edge of food trends. Provide continuous training to ensure the members of the chef's team are capable of handling all the preparation responsibilities. This will allow the chef to step aside to measure and monitor the effectiveness of the system. He or she can determine whether the processes and procedures that have been developed meet department objectives from the four food-service perspectives. Moreover, this enables a constant tweaking of the processes, like a recipe, to get the right blend of speed and accuracy in assembly and presentation. It'll help the chef to ensure a good workflow, *mise en place*, and workstation layout and to eliminate certain dishes and create new ones to match the available space and equipment.

Working with the person the chef has to designated to do the ordering will be the next order of business.

Stewarding Scorecard Objective and Measures

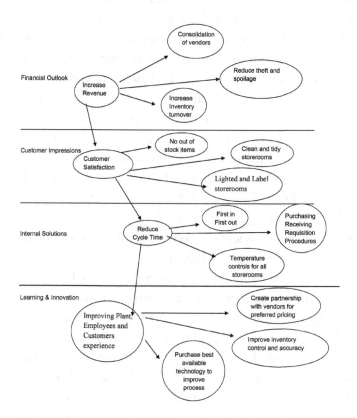

Diagram #14: Department Scorecard

## Purchasing scorecard

It's imperative to find suitable ingredients and supplies at a good price. This department's mission is to purchase ingredients for their intended use, in collaboration with the chef of course. When you're considering profit, for example, tomatoes that will be used in any salad, where appearance is important, need not to be of the same quality as those to be used in a sauce. In food-service operations, the launching point of the financial cycle is maintaining a great relationship with all your vendors. That will keep you abreast of market conditions for ingredients and changing trends and prices so you can communicate with the chef to plan menus accordingly.

Another critical aspect of purchasing to keep in mind is the fact that most ingredients used in a restaurant kitchen are also used by your employees in their homes. Purchase specifications should be in sizes that would be difficult to conceal and remove from your restaurant. At the same time, purchase quantities must be guided by the frequency of vendors' deliveries, as well as safety factors. Focus on keeping the inventory low, the turnover high, and waste and spoilage to a bare minimum. That will keep you on track to be lean and flexible and to adjust for current market trends and cost.

There is no easy way to streamline your purchasing choices, as prices change frequently. Likewise, availability and quality are both constantly changing. This is just as true for the likelihood of a super vendor emerging as your primary supplier. It's best to establish relationships with vendors from whom you can get as many ingredients as possible, to your specifications, vendors who offer best prices and a long-term mutual agreement that ensures a win-win situation. Procuring fresh quality products and ensuring that they are properly received, stored, issued, and used requires well-established processes and procedures and close monitoring. The application of software programs like ChefTec to simplify is critical. And where possible, get protection from adverse market conditions.

Be sure to discuss and agree upon terms of agreements. The pricing should be competitive, and specifications should include quality of the product, time of delivery, time of payment, and return policy. Establish credit terms, par stocks (a reasonable amount of an item to have on hand) and reorder points (a point that triggers reordering when supply of a certain item falls below the par stock amount). Then you can seamlessly integrate your data with your supplier, which will equal time saving.

Have one or two alternate suppliers that you can contact for comparison to keep your primary supplier honest.

Usually it is the responsibility of the chef or someone the chef designates to place orders and receive supplies. That person will also have the authority to reject delivery of substandard items. Make sure that the person ordering is different from the person receiving. This will reduce collusions. Decide on optimal delivery size to reduce cost of delivery and handling. Next, set a time window for delivery that allows the receiver to give his or her undivided attention to this activity. After all, here at the back door is where your profit cycle begins—a cycle that continues to the cash register and then to your bank account or back out both doors without proper check-and-balance control points.

Lastly, check all deliveries for quality, quantity, weight, price, and other variables to your specifications to eliminate surprises, and store products immediately. Information collected in your purchasing cycle now becomes data for cost-control analytics.

Savvy operators should be on the lookout for suppliers who want to par up your restaurant in order to move items sitting on their warehouse shelves. To rephrase differently, remember that suppliers are in the business of selling food, beverages, and related items to restaurants and will likely attempt to sell whatever they have on hand. Inventory represents money that draws no interest and serves no useful purpose sitting on your storeroom shelves and in your refrigerators when it could be in your bank account earning interest.

Part of the purchasing system ensures that food items and other supplies are stored so that they fit into overall system. This means that storage should be arranged for easy receiving, easy issuing, and easy inventory control. In the dry goods storeroom, canned, packaged, and bulk dry food are stored according to usage. The most-used foods are stored closest to the door, with the least-used items in less accessible locations.

Once a system of storage has been arranged and the items stored according to usage, create a form that lists the items in the sequence in which they are stored. The form will be used to take physical inventory.

As foods are received, they are stored at the back of shelves, and the older items are moved forward to be used first. This rotational system helps assure that items are not allowed to become too old, expire, and become unusable. Such waste adds to your food cost.

In costing an inventory, the last-in, first-out (LIFO) system costs the items at the price paid for the last purchased. The first-in, first-out (FIFO) system uses the price actually paid for the item. During a period of inflation, the two costs could be quite different. Whichever method is used, it must be used consistently.

Finally, keep a clean, tidy, well-labeled, well-lit, temperature-controlled storeroom to avoid unnecessary purchases. These steps will support your first-in, first-out (FIFO) rotation system and increase the accuracy of your inventory count. So when you are ready to apply technology to the count-and-requisition system, it will be a smooth transition.

Regardless of the strength of the relationship you have with your vendors—including the salesman, truck driver, or loader—you still have to check and verify every purchase order when its delivered to your back door. Check for accuracy in weight, size, count, quality, and whatever variable specification you requested on the purchase order. I'm reminded of a saying; "in every deal there is *a sucker.*"

*Please don't be the sucker.* I can't remember who it was who said this to me at a networking event, but it's appropriate to repeat it now. It is certainly applicable here, as deliveries are always full of surprises. Diagram 13 above is your visual image for success in purchasing.

# CONCLUSION

In the food-service industry the margins are thinner than a single piece of linguini pasta. And it's labor intensive. That's no secret. The cost of labor is now the biggest factor that threatens the sustainability of our industry. Some of the most successful independent operators stumbled into the industry, rather than having purposefully pursued it by choice. The unintentional consequences have given rise to a different perspective—one that's broadened the view of what food service (and, by extension, restaurants and hospitality) should be. It is equal parts food and entertainment and theatrics, with mood-inducing lighting designed to increase hospitality and enable sociability for all.

Managers too must expand their role to include physiologist, statistician, marketer, conductor, coach, and chief strategy officer in order to increase their value to their organization. The ability to flip the switch from one role to the next should come as naturally as the smile on the manager's face. To counter the external forces at the intersection of trends, technology, data collection, consumer behavior, and communication and to enable you to make decisions that enhance the effectiveness of your unique circumstances, use the analytical tools presented here to measure everything you manage.

Given all we've presented and the challenges that lie ahead, it's clear that a balanced approach to management is the best way to provide stability in an unstable environment. This systematic approach focuses on four areas of operation management. Within each, you can choose measures that will enable you to manage and to attain your financial goals.

Unsystematic risk in one perspective can be mitigated through improvements in the other three. For example, as of this writing, increases in minimum wages in some cities, such as Seattle, Los Angles, and New York, have made the state minimum wage higher than the federal minimum wage. Mandates by state laws can be offset by a combination of increase in productivity; reduction in waste, spoilage, and shrinkage; and use of technology. Increase in prices remains an option you can turn to as a last resort.

The effect of objectives is caused by the measures, and the measures are correlated to each other. The strength of the correlation is determined by the number of measures. The more measures used, the stronger the correlation. A measure by itself does not prove effective enough to cause an objective to occur. As an example, let's look at an increase in sales of bottled water, the effect, with sales of bottle water being a dependent variable. Let's say the increase is caused by high temperatures of one hundred degrees or more, with temperatures over one hundred degrees as an independent variable. Looking at the two variables alone is not proof of a cause-and-effect relationship—unless the sales occur in a desert with only one place that sells bottled water. Customers purchase bottled water in the desert because the temperature is over one hundred degrees, and there is no other place to purchase bottled water when they are thirsty. End of story. In the real world, there are many independent variables—measures to choose from to determine cause-and-effect relationships when it comes to meeting your operational goals. Go ahead—decide what your goals are, and choose measures that best fit the achievement of those goals. Then go out there in the dining room, kitchen, loading dock, or storeroom, and get on the telephone to your suppliers and prove it. A successful restaurant can never be run remotely by an absentee owner, even with a great general manager. Everyone—from the pot washer to the general manager—must lean in together, in alignment with one purpose, translated to individual tasks.

What this writing has set out to prove is that a balanced approach to food-service management is best. It's not a fashion trend or fad that will go out of style. It's not a flavor-of-the-month beverage or ice cream that will make your sales explode one month and then die a natural death the next month. *A Balanced Approach to Restaurant Management* is not a get-rich-quick book. Read it, and you can turn your restaurant into a highly successful one. I am not selling fear of failure because of the significant high rate of closures. I seek to inform and inspire those who set out on this journey to recalibrate the scale and scope of what food service is now and what it will be in the future. It will always be structured on the four foundational pillars of employees and customer impressions, internal solutions, financial outlook, and learning and development. There are no identical twins. You set goals for each area and create measures to achieve them. Use the gift of feedback from your employees, customers, and suppliers to continuously improve and strengthen the feedback loop.

The cause-and-effect relationship among the four perspectives—and, thus, the measures and goals and processes and procedures established for each—is well established. These segments are so strongly bundled together—so interdependent and interrelated—that every task, every individual action in one segment, is aligned to a measurable process and procedure (based on a goal) that has an effect on the other three.

The only guaranteed way to improve your bottom line is to continuously improve the processes, putting new measures in place as soon as learning occurs from feedback. Feedback is the most reliable path to improvement. Feedback is also the best way to discover your strengths. Operators need an open channel of communication with employees and customers. This open dialogue leads to greater candor in directions, enhancing credibility and competency on both sides. It shows that you care. There is too much randomness, uncertainty, and unpredictability in the food-service industry. Yet it is on this uncertainty that operators thrive. Believing that you will succeed if your operation is based on a fifty-fifty coin toss—a daily hope for a positive random act to occur—is wishful thinking. It is better to collect as much information about the customers you serve as you can and study the data in order to predict future behavior or at least create offers and opportunities that will entice customers to return more often. *A Balanced Approach to Restaurant Management* provides a toolbox of techniques that will enable you to take a fresh look at your operation.

This approach combines academic rigor with proven operational expertise in best practices, a link that has been proven by established authors over the previous two decades.

There you have it. Now go with confidence into your kitchen, dining room, and storeroom, and create your own scorecard using a balanced approach weighted toward the critical success factors of your restaurant.

# ENDNOTES

1   Robert S. Kaplan and David Norton, "The Balanced Score Card: Measures That Drive Performance," *Harvard Business Review,* 70, no. 1 (January/February 1992).

2   Bruce Serlen, *Hotel Business,* 20, March 7, 2011.

3   H. G. Parsa, John T. Self, David Njite, and Tiffany King, "Why Restaurants Fail," *Cornell Hospitality Quarterly,* 46 (3), 304–322. Self (2004) Restaurant Failure rate.

4   Eugene W. Anderson and Mary W. Sullivan, "The Antecedents and Consequences of Customer Satisfaction for Firms," *Marketing Science,* 12, no. 2 (1993): 125–143.

5   Richard Federico, Corporate Leadership Council, "Linking Employee Satisfaction with Productivity, Performance, and Customer Satisfaction," July 2003, http://www.keepem.com/doc_files/ clc_articl_on_productivity.pdf.

6   Benjamin Schneider, Paul J. Hanges, D. Brent Smith, and Amy Nichole Salvaggio, Survey of satisfaction levels of bank customers and employees, in "Which Comes First: Employee Attitudes or Organizational Financial and Market Performance?" *Journal of Applied Psychology,* 88, no. 5 (1980): 836–851.

7   Frederick Reicheld, *The Loyalty Effect: The Hidden Force behind Growth, Profits, and Lasting Value* (Boston: Bain & Company, Inc., 1996).

8   W. Earl Sasser, Leonard A. Schlesinger, and James L. Heskett, *The Service Profit Chain: How Leading Companies Link Profit and Growth to Loyalty, Satisfaction, and Value* (Simon and Schuster, 1997).

9   Dr. Thomas Rollins of the Hay Group, Corporate Executive Board, July 2003 (www.corporateleadershipcouncil.com), developed a model linking

employee opinion survey results directly with business performance metrics.

10  Learn more about ChefTec at www.cheftec.com.

11  See https://en.wikipedia.org/wiki/Predictive_modelling.

Printed in the United States
By Bookmasters